Keep on
Romancing

Andrea
Guillernel ♡

AN INSIDER'S GUIDE FOR COUPLES

Written by **Autumn Millhouse**

Edited by **Christina Luce**

Published by **Romantic Travel Publishing**

Dedicated to my Dad

ROMANTIC NAPA VALLEY: AN INSIDER'S GUIDE FOR COUPLES, FIRST EDITION

Written by Autumn Millhouse

Copyright 2008 by Romantic Travel Publishing
All Rights Reserved.

Published by Romantic Travel Publishing
3379 Solano Avenue, # 400
Napa, California 94559 U.S.A.
707.227.4152
wwww.romantictravelpublishing.com

Cover Picture by John Klycinski, Orlando & Angela Engagement Photo,
Veterans Home, Yountville, CA.

Designed by Houston&, Atlanta, Georgia USA, www.houstonand.com

For further information, discounted bulk rates, or to be included in our Second
Edition, please contact Romantic Travel Publishing

www.romanticnapavalleybook.com

ISBN # 978-0-9815881-0-0
Printed in Singapore

TABLE OF CONTENTS

Wine Sip

If you were a vintage bottle of wine
And I could fill my cup
I'd savor your essence for a time
Then slowly I'd drink you up
I'd let you linger on my tongue
Delight my palate with your bouquet
My lips would bathe in your crimson pool
And I'd sit and sip all day
If you were a vintage bottle of wine
All mellow and aged in wood
I'd whirl you and swirl you around my mouth
And hold you as long as I could
I'd drink from you slowly and deeply,
And make your flavor last,
I would not stop, till the very last drop
And I'd probably lick my glass

— *author unknown*

BOB HURLEY
Owner of Hurley's Restaurant

FOREWORD

by Bob Hurley

I've done a fair amount of traveling in my life – and not just short-term vacation and business trips, but real, honest-to-God "I'll see you in a couple of years" travel. My wife Cynthia and I have been lucky enough to see much of Europe, even living for a while in Switzerland and the South of France. We've also made our way through North Africa, India and most of Southeast Asia, and always managed to do it in style. I can't begin to count the number of times my wife has shifted her gaze from some amazing vista to look up at me and say, "Isn't this romantic?"

But even the most avid travelers need a place to call home, and when we landed in Napa Valley, we knew we'd found ours. Twenty years, two kids, and a very demanding restaurant later, I still find Cynthia whispering those same words to me from atop some beautiful Napa hillside or other: "Isn't this romantic?" Indeed, this place is as romantic as it gets.

At Hurley's, I spend a good deal of my time keeping things in perfect balance. For example, the menu must remain balanced, reflecting both my personal tastes as well as those of our patrons. The food itself presents a very delicate balance of flavors and textures – of course, once you add wine into the mix, a whole new balancing act ensues, one that requires much patience and a great deal of passion. Life is like that too, and well-balanced living demands a generous helping of romance. In this increasingly busy and high-pressured world, to deprive oneself of those most precious moments on earth is to deny the most fundamental needs common to each and every one of us.

In the pages that follow, you will find a very special Napa Valley handed down to you by a true romantic and longtime native. With millions of people passing through each year and so much to see, Autumn's book will help you discover your own favorite corners and secret romantic spots. So place this little treasure into the hands of your lover or spouse as you announce surprise plans for a trip to the wine country, and enjoy the ride.

Happy Travels, Bob Hurley

Romantic Napa Valley

INTRODUCTION

Sharing the beauty of Napa Valley has been a passion of mine for years, so it was no great surprise when I began to feel a tug on my heartstrings to write this book. A third-generation Napan, I grew up knowing that my home was a very special place; however, as is often the case, I didn't realize just how special it was until I left it. By the time I came to my senses and returned in my late twenties, the Valley had been transformed: the popularity of wine had skyrocketed among the masses, and wine tasting in the Valley had become an internationally-favored pastime!

I want to show you the best that Napa Valley has to offer — from an insider's perspective. While a few local travel guides and magazines highlight a limited selection of wineries and restaurants, such "local" sources are based on solicited recommendations by non-locals for commercial reasons. Romantic Napa Valley is entirely different, as you will see. I have compiled recommendations for the most amazing experiences possible, free of commercial influence. This book is the pure product of my authentic, knowledgeable opinion, plain and simple. My findings are accumulated over three decades of living and breathing this place — everything I adore most about the Valley, and all the places I would take my own lover or best friend, I now pass on to you. Although this book is tailored for those seeking romance, it can also serve well for a girls' weekend away or a relaxing weekend on your own. Whatever your purpose, you will treasure the experience for many years to come.

Inside you will find the most enchanting wineries, mouth-watering restaurants, beautiful accommodations, breathtaking spots to pop the question, and practical wine-tasting etiquette. These pages are filled with hidden gems you will never hear about otherwise. Many locals won't tell you about them, and some can be difficult to find without reliable guidance, especially when you're trying to filter through the over 300 wineries in Napa County. Navigating the Valley to see as much as possible in a short amount of time requires some insight to effectively manage your time and resources. My sample itineraries provide plans for the most fun and romantic trips possible. Of course, when you are with the right person, any place can be romantic…but my recommendations will provide some much needed assistance to accessing a wealth of seductive beauty inherent to the Valley – if you know where to look!

When choosing which places to deem the most romantic, I asked myself a variety of questions, including: Is it personalized and tasteful, or is it so well-known that it is constantly overrun by tourism? Are the owners and staff not only experts in the field, but also friendly and welcoming, or is there a note of wine-snobbery in the air? Are there beautiful natural surroundings, and is the atmosphere conducive to spontaneous acts of romance? Is it reasonably affordable, while retaining a sense of luxury? Are there special qualities that no other place like it has? Those were the questions; now here are the answers. I give you the most romantic establishments in Napa Valley!

Keep on Romancing,

Autumn

AUTUMN MILLHOUSE
Author of Romantic Napa Valley

Chapter One

NAPA VALLEY'S

ROMANTIC APPEAL

AUTUMN VINEYARDS, NAPA

NAPA VALLEY'S ROMANTIC APPEAL

It was my nineteenth birthday. My heart sang as I sped past the vines on the back of Sam's motorcycle, clinging to him for dear life and loving every minute of it. I had grown up in the Valley, but never had it exuded such magic as it did that day. The winding roads seemed more exhilarating, the colors appeared more vivid, and the smell of the sun on the grapes filled my senses with more sweetness than it ever had.

The Valley had been working its subtle magic on us all summer, and on that particular day, I felt as if I could accomplish anything (even my Chemistry midterm). Sam had signed my birthday card with "Love," and both of us, young as we were, knew exactly what that meant. He was mine, and I was his.

As I remember that day now, I feel again that the palpable romantic quality of the Valley is timeless. Napa is a veritable Shangri-La hidden among rolling green hills and endless vineyards. Its sensual and endlessly indulgent arrows of Cupid will target all of your five senses.

Some say that if they had to choose between sex and a great massage, they would choose the massage. But I say: you're in Napa! Why limit yourself? Indulge in a salt scrub, a mud bath, and a couple's massage, all within reach of your loved one's hand.

jaimefritsch.com

O'BRIEN FAMILY WINERY

Your eyes will wander everywhere and take in everything – the dramatic winescapes, the hillsides, the Victorian buildings. But the best sight by far will be your lover's smile as you explore this Eden together.

Listen—what do you hear? Is it the sound of hot air balloons heaving above you, waiting to whisk you both into the clouds? Or is it merely your heart beating in anticipation as the cork pops on a new vintage?

In summer, you can smell the heat of the Valley enlivening its massive, fragrant eucalyptus trees. You can sample thousands of wine varietals, then inhale the bouquet of our world-famous Cabernets and Merlots. Use the wine wheel to discover easy ways to remember and describe specific qualities of wine. These myriad scents will bring you right back to Napa when you uncork your new finds at home. If your taste buds yearn for more than wine, add some caviar and chocolate to the mix. Overindulge a bit.

The Valley is so romantic, sensual, and stylish that until recently, many of the locals hoped to keep it under wraps – but no such luck. Over the past decade, as the international cult of wine has skyrocketed, the Valley has become a Mecca for celebrities, wine connoisseurs and plain old drunks – wealthy ones, of course.

In my grandparents' and great-grandparents' time, Napa County was a rural farm area. It was almost entirely devoted to fruit orchards, livestock and dairying. The first winery, Charles Krug, was built in 1861 and is still in operation today. With the revolutionary victory at the Paris Wine Tasting of 1976 – when nine Parisian wine experts chose Napa wine over France's own Cabernet Sauvignon – the beautiful Valley I love to call home gained international acclaim.

Now, five million lucky souls visit our Valley every year. Napa County has been called the most lovely, most fertile, and most favored land in the West. Most places here close up shop by ten in the evening, and you can stroll down the quiet, serene streets at ease, feeling like the only two people in the world.

WINE COUNTRY LIVING

How did the American concept of wine country living originate? From the 1960's on, Robert Mondavi's winery has epitomized the kind of gracious hospitality that makes every visitor feel like one of the family. The Mondavi Family even paved the way for a wider selection of winery event hosting: now there are tours, concerts, picnicking, public education, cooking demonstrations, and art exhibits, which continue to draw ever larger and more appreciative crowds to linger, taste and buy.

Our Valley carries the cachet of wealth; it is the most affluent county in California proportionate to size. No longer considered an obscure hideaway, its prestigious mystique has drawn Silicon Valley tycoons, trophy wine entrepreneurs, and world-renowned celebrities to this delicious destination.

In fact, if Hollywood built a movie set called "Hedonist's Eden," it would look like wine country. The entertainment industry has chosen our Valley as a backdrop for many successful productions, such as *A Walk in the Clouds* and *Falcon Crest*. Elvis Presley was one the first celebrities to visit and film in the Valley, and many others have followed him. Sweethearts Jake Gyllenhaal and Reese Witherspoon even left Italy to pay romantic homage to Napa Valley. Marcia Cross of *Desperate Housewives* is rumored to have become engaged to her husband here, and Christina Aguilera tied the knot against the Valley's naturally stunning backdrop. Robert Redford, Joe Montana and Robin Williams own homes here, and even Rudy Giuliani and Hillary Clinton have dropped in for a little wine tasting and positive exposure. Celebrities such as Jeff Gordon and Vince Neil have taken the initiative to create their own private wine labels and inspire their own vintages. Mario Andretti and Francis Ford Coppola have their own wineries, and are often spotted enjoying their own wine al fresco.

jaimefritsch.com

CHATAEU POTELLE

While there are vineyards all over the world, the phrase "Wine Country Living" has become synonymous with Napa Valley. One can watch a cooking show called "Easy Entertaining," filmed in Napa by Michael Chiarello for Food Network, or "In Wine Country," which promotes the essence of wine country living, including the participatory cooking classes and local wine competitions. This kind of media perpetuates the relaxing, stylish comfort that wine country living encompasses.

Why has the Napa Valley so often been compared with St. Tropez, France's luxury getaway? The philosophy of the French café culture is to revel in *la douce vie* (the soft life) and promote *joie de vivre* (the joy of life) through deep conversations, introspection, appreciation of one's surroundings, taking pleasure in simple yet decadent meals, and flavorful, sophisticated wines. Similarly, our enchanted Valley beckons visitors to partake of its luxurious beauty and indulgent lifestyle, if only for a weekend.

Wine country living eludes absolute description. It is casual, yet refined. It is a mélange of fine wines, impeccable cuisines, and sensual surroundings, topped off by a simple approach to living. Combine the ease of a Mediterranean climate with a soupcon of Parisian elitism, add a dash of L.A. glamour and a dollop of Cali beach bum. Stir in laughter, wine, friendship and romance. *Voilà*, wine country living!

What is it about wine country that makes visitors feel like family? You arrive in town on Friday, not knowing a soul. By Sunday afternoon, you're on a first-name basis with winery owners and shopkeepers. Locals have a wealth of historical knowledge about the area, more accurate than any concierge's. The small-town feeling and friendly locals will make any city folk open their hearts and desire to move here by the weekend's close.

Napa Valley is the place to live out the old clichés and make them yours. *Carpe diem.* Eat, drink and be merry. Live your life fully and completely. Love without reservation. Enjoy all that the world has to offer.

While franchises and developers may reach toward our Valley paradise, nothing can spoil it. In 1968, to prevent suburban sprawl, Napa Valley became a mandated agricultural preserve. Valley home sites were limited to at least 40 acres, and hillside sites to 160. The county also mandates a slow-growth policy with the most growth occurring in recent years. Consequently, locals hope to see the Valley continue to keep its charm and small-town feel.

As long as wine remains a popular and ever-growing enterprise, and as long as winemakers revel in the joy of their admirable professions, there will be exquisite wineries. And where there are exquisite wines, couples will come to stroll, sip and savor the tastings, along with each other's company. Wine is always better with the one you love. The very essence of the Valley calls for passion and joy, whether you bring these qualities with you, or discover them in yourself here – either way, you can be sure that your personal *élan* will be enhanced during your stay.

So sit back, cuddle up with your lover, and plan your Napa Valley getaway. Everything your senses desire is right here.

Romantic Napa Valley

Chapter two

INSIDE

NAPA VALLEY

NAPA | MÉLANGE OF MAIN STREET

Driving into Napa might not be what you expect. Ignore the south end and its big box stores. Once you reach downtown, you will start to get a taste of the true town character.

Napa is the largest city in the Valley and is where most of the locals reside. Downtown is the star of Napa and often serves as the hot spot for tourists and locals alike. Victorian homes, often serving as cute Bed & Breakfasts, ring the perimeters, while the heart of downtown is filled with award-winning restaurants, galleries, wine tasting bars and shopping. It's the location that serves as the hub for many community events as well, such as the Chef's Market, Napa's Annual Christmas Parade and Fourth of July's Symphony on the River.

Downtown at the end of South Main Street is the **Napa Mill,** the largest redevelopment project in Napa history, incorporating a $238 million flood-control plan. The Napa Mill incorporates many other shops, including the historic **Hatt building**, restaurants and galleries such as the **General Store, Sweetie Pies** and **Celedon**. The wraparound river walk is still under construction with a highly anticipated opening in the near future.

Copia, the American Center for Wine, Food and the Arts is Napa's new cultural epicenter. Learn about the role of wine and food in our culture. Watch cooking demonstrations, taste wine and walk the outside gardens. Even catch a film in the outdoor amphitheater. Behind Copia runs a hiking trail along the Napa River that will be 12 miles long when completed and is a great way to walk off the crème brûlée from **Julia's Kitchen**. Next to Copia is the **Oxbow Public Market**, a 40,000 square foot market that sells local gourmet edibles. Enjoy a French style cheese shop, an endless array of wine, and shop at **Kitchen Library**, Napa Valley, where you can discover a hard-to-find object of art that evokes a sense of adventure.

AERIAL VIEW OF NAPA MILL

Downtown Napa offers more than a dozen or so wine tasting rooms, all within walking distance of one another, which will save you from trekking around the Valley. Some of the most popular are **Vintner's Collective, Rocca** and **Back Room Wines**. This is a great way to taste local varietals in an efficient amount of time. Usually the wines are from smaller unknown wineries which allow you to find a new favorite wine.

jaimefritsch.com

Take a yoga class at **Ubuntu**, which boasts a "vegetable cuisine" downstairs and yoga classes upstairs. Before you start a day of wine tasting, begin with a Wake Up & Flow class or end your day with Yoga Happy Hour.

The Napa Opera House, known as the "Jewel of the Valley", was built in 1879 and restored 120 years later. Today it houses everything from live comedy to world music, to contemporary theatre. Book your tickets in advance so you can enjoy a show after a savory meal at an award winning restaurant downtown, such as **Cole's Chop House**.

Celebrity Sightings: Reece Witherspoon, Jake Gyllenhaal, Jason Priestley, Gene Simmons, Matt Damon, Mario Andretti, Stevie Wonder, Jeff Gordon, Danielle Steel, Sean Pean, Keanu Reeves, Jerry Rice and Bill Clinton.

Origins: Originally, the first settlers of the Napa Valley were the Native American tribe, the Wappo Indians. The legend is that the name is derived from the Spanish word Guapo because of their intense resistance to the Mexican explorers. Native Napans believe that the Indians cursed the land so that locals will always return.

ALAN SHEPP'S MOSAIC FOUNTAIN, NAPA MILL

Returning home is never a surprise. "You always do" is often the response. Napa was always the county seat of wine country. The boundaries were planted in beans in 1847, and Nathan Coombs laid out the town the following year. He originally wanted to name the town Coombsville, but the name didn't last. The first building was (naturally) a saloon.

The California gold strike 100 miles away temporarily slowed down Napa's development, but soon discouraged miners streamed into town and became its early settlers. The Napa River provided access to commerce from San Francisco and downtown developed quickly.

What makes Yountville so decadent? Let us count the ways. For one thing, you can choose from the largest number of fine dining establishments per capita in the entire U.S. Most notably, and continually rated one the best restaurants in the world, is **The French Laundry.**

Perched on the west side of the town is the largest and oldest **Veterans Home,** filled with honorable war heroes. **The Napa Valley Museum** is located onsite as well, whose mission is to enlighten and inspire visitors from near and far about the Valley's contributions, most notably in wine.

The Veterans Home also houses Yountville's **Lincoln Theater.** The Theatre just turned 50, and got a grand $20 million facelift. Here you can witness Broadway spectacles, holiday favorites and top-notch international performers. If tickets are not available, feel free to enjoy the lively blues at **Pacific Blues Café** most Saturdays.

An early winery, built by the Groezingers in 1874, thrives today as a massive stone compound called **V Marketplace** (formerly Vintage 1870). Filled with art galleries, wine and luxury shops, it is a great host to many events throughout the year, such as Taste of Yountville, Halloween Spooktacular and Father's Day Invitational Auto Show. Take a nice stroll with your morning coffee and croissant from **Bouchon Bakery** to explore the property.

Yountville hosts an annual Festival of Lights, in which many local wineries participate. Picture thousands of lights twinkling on a crisp November evening. Sample wine, ride in old-fashioned carriages and visit Saint Nick.

Celebrity Sightings: Christina Aguilera, Robin Williams, Alicia Silverstone, Rudy Giuliani, Drew Barrymore, Ben Affleck, Jessica Simpson and Nick Lachey.

Origins: Yountville has a very unusual history. The Napa Valley was Mexican property when George C. Yount came on the scene in 1836. He was the only white settler to own land and live in the Napa Valley for many years. He was said to have been friends with the Wappo tribe who inhabited his land, until small pox eradicated most of the Indians years later. Yount was the first American to receive a Spanish land grant to build the town and originally named it Sebastopol, until his fellow neighbors renamed the town in his honor in 1869.

ST. HELENA | THE HEART OF NAPA VALLEY

Located at the geographical center of the Valley, St. Helena produces some of Napa's finest wines. Greystone, a castle that once housed the Christian Brothers Winery, is now the **Culinary Institute of America**. Explore the breathtaking property, enjoy their fine dining establishment or enjoy a Culinary Cooking Demonstration. Next to CIA is a St. Helena historic landmark, **Beringer Winery**, which has operated continuously since 1876, no small feat during Prohibition.

St. Helena is a combination of country charm and sophisticated chic. Pick up a freshly roasted cup of coffee from the **Napa Valley Roasting Company** and explore the town on foot. Main Street has everything your heart desires: jewelry, housewares, clothing and decadent edibles. It even hosts the Hometown Harvest Festival, featuring a pet parade, music and wine tasting, of course.

Highlighted on the Food Network, **Taylor's Refresher** is a classic drive-in transformed into a nouvelle eatery. From the Ahi Tuna burgers to their sweet potato fries, they please thousands of hungry visitors each year with their modern twist on American classics. In 2006 they were awarded an American Classic Restaurant Winner by the James Beard Foundation.

The hugely popular Auction Napa Valley is an annual Napa Valley signature event—a food and wine festival. Held each year at **Meadowwood Resort**, this event is invitation only and is often hosted by celebrities, such as past hosts Dana Carvey and Ryan Seacrest. There are a series of events that precede the actual event and draws world wide wine aficionados and celebrities. Year after year the event becomes more well known and successful. In 2006 the auction raised over 9 million dollars for charity.

COOK RESTAURANT

jaimefritsch.com

MARTINI HOUSE &
TAYLOR'S REFRESHER

Celebrity Sightings: Geena Davis, Jennifer & Joe Montana, Robert Redford, Dana Carvey, Hillary Clinton, Ryan Seacrest, Alicia Silverstone.

Origins: Edward Bale bought the land that was destined to become St. Helena from the Mexican government. His **Bale Grist Mill** dates from 1846, and was instrumental in Napa Valley's settlement. It still operates today and is a fascinating sight to explore.

Robert Louis Stevenson, author of *Treasure Island* and *Kidnapped*, has lent his distinguished name to a number of St. Helena landmarks, including a Stevenson monument. Robert Louis Stevenson State Park dates from 1880, and was named for the famous author after he spent his honeymoon there researching a book about Mount St. Helena.

RUTHERFORD & OAKVILLE | HEARTBEAT AWAY

If you blink you may very well miss these tiny, yet interesting towns. They are worth mentioning because of their appealing charm, historical significance and merit today. Rutherford is named after George C. Yount's son-in-law, Thomas Rutherford.

Today they have earned recognition as award winning wine growing regions, and have a slew of amazing wineries such as **Rubicon Estate, Opus One** and **Silver Oak Cellars**. Other popular tourist destinations are **St. Helena Olive Oil Company, Oakville Grocery** and **Rutherford Grill**.

CALISTOGA | SOAK, PAMPER AND REJUVENATE

Talk about a blast from the past. You can't get to Calistoga by freeway. Modern day Calistoga features a pedestrian-friendly downtown, and a "no fast food" mandate. The National Trust for Historic Preservation officially dubbed it a Distinctive Destination in 2001.

Calistoga looks down on the rest of the valley as the undisputed queen of health and vitality. She boasts no less than a dozen spas and natural hot springs, most notably **Dr. Wilkins**. The Wappo Indians used the springs for spiritual and medicinal purposes for thousands of years.

A notable Calistoga trademark is **Calistoga Sparking Water**, which is also sourced from the rich natural springs of the Valley. The facilities are located along Silverado Trail right before you enter Calistoga.

Attend the Napa County Fair in July, or Old Mill Days in October at Bale Grist Mill Historic Park. The **Calistoga Farmers Market** offers farm-fresh vegetables, seasonal fruits and live entertainment. The Fall Napa Valley Blues Festival marks the end of crush and features dozens of wineries, talented Blues bands and **Busters Original Southern BBQ**. The restored 1862 **Schramsberg Winery** was the first hillside winery in the Napa Valley. Today the winery is known for its amazing sparkling wine and welcomes guests by appointment.

Mount St. Helena, an extinct volcano, overlooks **Robert Louis Stevenson State Park**. It's one of the few Bay Area peaks to accumulate winter snow-fall. The challenging five-mile hike to the summit will reward you with panoramic vistas.

Celebrity Sightings: Mick Jagger, Bono, Vince Neil, Marcia Cross, Steven Spielberg, Tyra Banks, Michelle Pfeiffer and Jessica Biel.

SOLAGE

Origins: 150 years ago, the Napa Valley's first hedonistic seeds were sown. "Taking the waters" became the health seeker's fad, and nouveau riche Americans flocked here. Calistoga was the original fashionable West Coast spa destination.

Sam Brannan, California's first millionaire and a Vigilante, purchased the springs in 1859, and was instrumental in bringing the transcontinental railroad into Calistoga.

The **Indian Springs Resort and Spa** now stands on Brannan's old property, and you can still visit the one remaining 1866 cottage from the original resort. Today Brannan's 1868 Depot is the second oldest remaining train station in California. Antique railroad cars house tiny boutiques on the main street of town.

AUTUMN VINEYARDS, RUTHERFORD

Chapter Three

WINE COUNTRY

WEEKEND SOJOURNS

ATTENTION DOG AND WINE LOVERS

FRIDAY
ACCOMMODATIONS | THE MERITAGE RESORT AT NAPA

Recently constructed (2006) and located on the southern tip of Napa, this dog-friendly resort features a spa, restaurant, and bar. Since wine tasting can sometimes be exhausting, this plentiful haven is the perfect place to relax. Sip wine at their Private Caves; enjoy a couple's massage in the luxurious Cave spa; enjoy nightcap cocktails before the lobby's roaring fireplace or around the outdoor fire pit, while admiring the lighted hillside vineyard and Our Lady of the Grapes statue.

Start your stay with the **Meritage's** Wine Tasting welcome on Thursday & Friday evenings and make sure to utilize their shuttle service for your first night on the town. If venturing out isn't in the cards for you, enjoy your vino in the hot tub and dine at the resort's Italian restaurant, **Siena.**

Before venturing out, have the concierge make a reservation at Ristorante Allegria, a local romantic favorite. Enjoy my favorite skirt steak or Napa Cabbage salad, and don't forget to share the bread pudding for dessert. If you are ready for more after dinner, walk two blocks down Main Street to **Uva Trattoria Italiana** for a nightcap and some jazz. They quiet down early, so make sure to get there in time to enjoy the last set. If that hasn't quenched your nightlife thirst, walk back down to Main and First and hit a great local nighttime spot, **Bounty Hunter,** to savor one of their specialty rare wines.

SATURDAY
Taking into account the presence of your furry loved one, this day is planned so that you can go tasting in Napa Valley without leaving your pooch behind. The following wineries are dog-friendly, but keep in mind the possibility of special seasonal circumstances, such as busy production during Crush. Worst case scenario, you leave Fido in the car during a particular taste.

Also make sure to pick up the hugely popular book, *Winery Dogs of Napa Valley*, to find out more about the local dogs living at many wineries in the Valley. It is a neat experience to arrive knowing the name of the dog greeting you.

JELLYBEAN AT ACACIA WINERY
Courtesy of Winery Dogs of Napa Valley

MUMM NAPA

Note: the dog-friendly wineries I have chosen for this itinerary are among my favorite romantic ones, but there are quite a few others that also welcome dogs. Make sure to do your homework ahead of time if these recommendations don't suit you, and keep Fido out of places that discourage dogs, such as Chateau Potelle. Many wineries have resident dogs, so on a rare occasion bringing yours could create a disruption.

Before you start tasting, stop at **Vallergas Market** for a picnic lunch, including their famed Spinach dip. Important note: picnic at a winery where you plan to buy wine (picnic-friendly wineries included below). Do not bring your own wine or other alcohol with you — that is a HUGE *faux pas*.

The first dog-friendly winery is **Mumm Napa**. Located along the road less traveled, Silverado Trail, it is a beautiful drive anytime of the year. This picturesque patio setting is perfect for starting the day, especially while partaking in some sparkling wine. Try sharing the Mumm Sparkling Sampler, then decide on glasses to enjoy separately. Afterwards, move on to the renowned Photography Gallery that showcases classics like Ansel Adams.

Now head back toward Napa via Silverado Trail, stopping at **Regusci Winery.** At this "haunted" historical landmark built in 1876, you will be greeted by three rambunctious dogs. Enjoy the picturesque tasting facility, lovely views, bocce ball area, and manicured lawns for picnicking.

Further south on Silverado Trail is **Signorello Vineyards**, another beautiful winery perfect for your particular itinerary. Simply tasting at the wine bar with your dog is great, but reserving your Chocolate & Wine tasting ahead of time is even better — you will be able to enjoy the lovely patio, scenic views, and privileged seating. Imagine the decadence of mouth-watering chocolate and a luscious merlot to conclude your perfect day…

Dinner is a sensual experience at the **Farm Restaurant,** located at the Carneros Inn. The vibe is very hotel-chic; if you're from San Francisco, you will probably feel right at home. Cuddle up with a cocktail on the velvet couches while you wait to be seated, and then take pleasure in the luscious menu, featuring fresh and finely-combined dishes. After dinner, chill outside next to the modern fireplace and rest assured that you are creating memories that will last long after the conclusion of this trip.

SUNDAY

There is nothing like a lazy Sunday. After all the previous day's indulgence, refuel with a tasty Sunday Brunch. **Fume Bistro & Bar** is a local American bistro offering a charming atmosphere and tasty food at a great price. Their motto is "good food, always seasonally correct, great service & a comfortable seat." What more can you ask for? I've never been disappointed. Better yet, you can have your doggie with you as you feast on the patio. In chilly weather, they have heat lamps. The brunch menu is extensive, offering a variety of choices from omelets and breakfast pizzas to Fume chuck burgers and fresh salads.

After brunch, take some time to spoil your *chien* at **Alston Park,** located on Dry Creek Road, just across the freeway on the west end of the Valley. Get on Trower and cross the Freeway, and you will dead end into Dry Creek Road and Alston Park. Take a nice hike with your dog or allow him to play in the off-leash designated area.

Before you get jealous that your dog is having all the fun, I have one more special recommendation, described in greater detail in the winery section, which requires reservations. When you get back on Dry Creek Road, go North and take a right on Orchard Avenue where you will find the inherently romantic **O'Brien Estate Winery**. Barbie and Bart O'Brien create an intimate tasting experience and graciously allow your dog to join in. Enjoy the views, their wines, and even their comfy hammock in the back; they won't mind, trust me. Arrange a picnic lunch in advance if you like, and leave feeling like true members of the wine tasting community – a rarity in today's corporate wine culture.

AN EPICUREAN BIKE RIDE THROUGH STAGS LEAP

FRIDAY
ACCOMMODATIONS | VINTAGE INN

This charming Inn offers a Romantic Package that will generate magic for any couple. There is no better way to set the tone for a romantic weekend away than a haven like this, all tied up like a present. Per your request, a roaring fireplace, sunken bathtub for two, and crisp bottle of champagne could be included upon your arrival.

Located in adorable Yountville, there are many options to enjoy within close proximity. Start off with a classic French dinner at the highly acclaimed **Bistro Jeanty**. Owned by Phillip Jeanty, who you can find most nights conversing with local patrons from the kitchen window, this cozy, inviting restaurant is perfect for a rendezvous à deux. You will feel transported to a quaint village in the South of France. If reservations are hard to come by, you can always opt for cozy bar seating or enjoy the family-style tables in the front dining room. Either way, it will be *un bonsoir*!

If you're considering an aperitif after dinner and looking to enjoy some local recreation, go to the timeless **Pancha's,** which has been around so long that my great-grandpa use to drink there! It's an experience, so be open minded to talking and drinking with locals, who enjoy the pool tables and inexpensive drinks after their evening shifts.

SATURDAY

Working out is a must for me, but running a 5k isn't very appealing while on vacation. A compromise may be in order, what with all the delicious eating and drinking. So, after you have enjoyed your coffee and croissant from **Bouchon Bakery**, walk down to **Napa Valley Bike Tours & Rentals**; they have many tours for you to explore – a perfect combination of recreation and leisure.

Pick up a comfort bike for a self-guided day tour. Before starting out, call ahead to make reservations for lunch at **Robert Sinskey Vineyards**, a true epicurean treat featuring special food and wine pairing. Many wineries are moving beyond the traditional tasting to offer more to the cultivated wine connoisseur. At noon on Friday, Saturday and Sunday, the on-site chef takes you through an amazingly decadent wine and food pairing with the Bento Box.

jaimefritsch.com   STAGS LEAP APPELLATION

With this lunch reservation secured, head out to **Jessup Cellars** tasting room on Washington Street (near Napa Valley Bike Tours) to enjoy the wine and wonderful Volakis Gallery next store.

Now get back on your bikes and pedal for about 2 miles to arrive on time for your food pairing at noon. Going over Yountville crossroads, you will pass **Cliff Lede Vineyards**. This independently-owned winery focuses on Bordeaux varietal wines and hosts a beautiful art gallery. Another stop should be **Goosecross Cellars** at the end of State Lane, adjacent to Yountville Crossroads. This is a reputable and rustic homegrown winery with hospitable owners and staff specializing in Chardonnay and Cabernet Sauvignon.

If not exhausted from your bike riding adventure, I recommend a night of entertainment, wine country style. First enjoy dinner at **Bistro Don Giovanni,** a favorite Italian eatery. Check out the drink specials, share their famous fritto misto and lemon crème ravioli, or order a pizza fresh from wood burning ovens.

After dinner, check out the **Lincoln Theatre** or **Napa Valley Opera House** schedule. Both are newly renovated and boast world-class entertainment, from live comedy acts to Broadway hits like *Cats* or *Evita*. If you cannot get tickets in advance, I'd recommend checking in at will call or going online for possible availability.

SUNDAY

A huge fan of brunch and mimosas, I recommend walking through Yountville towards the Veterans Home to the **Vintner's Golf Club & Lakeside Grill** for brunch. The golf club is directly below the Vets home and has a beautifully landscaped course with a pond home to a family of swans. Sit outside and enjoy a casual meal, then play a competitive scramble or practice your swing on the golf range. The beautiful views can be distracting, so don't be surprised if you aren't up to par.

Domaine Chandon is one of my favorite wineries, though it is often packed with both tourists and locals due to the tapas-style food, yummy sparkling wine, and late hours. Nestled next to the Veterans Home, it appears hidden but is worth the visit. You can sit al fresco, which I prefer on summer days, or enjoy the hip lounge inside. They also possess a highly-acclaimed restaurant, **Étoile**, an upscale and memorable treat named after their popular pink sparkling wine.

FRIDAY
ACCOMMODATION | SILVERADO RESORT & SPA

This classic Napa resort offers many fabulous packages, but the Golf & Spa classic package fits perfectly into a weekend itinerary of leisure and recreation. **The Silverado Resort & Spa** has been around for as long as I can remember, always representing a magical sense of style and wine country sophistication. They have a world-renowned golf course, and recently added spa facilities. Silverado also offers three award-winning restaurants and an upbeat cocktail bar, making this itinerary ideal for groups of couples who want to get together for an entourage weekend.

I recommend exploring the on-site facilities your first evening in town. Enjoy dinner at any of the restaurants, and cocktails with live music. With hot air ballooning on the agenda for the next morning, you want to make this a leisurely, low key evening. Trust me — when you wake up at 5 a.m. the next day, you will be happy you stayed close by for an early night.

SILVERADO RESORT & SPA

BALLOONS ABOVE THE VALLEY

SATURDAY

As you wake early, you may feel a mixture of fear and excitement. A unique adventure awaits you! Prepare yourself for a once in a lifetime opportunity to enjoy a sunrise above one of the most beautiful locations in the world. There are several ballooning companies in the Valley, but my favorite is **Balloons Above the Valley**. You can't beat the endless opportunities for fun and romance with this company. Believe it or not, many of their skilled aviators are also certified ministers who have married numerous couples above the clouds, and orchestrated many other notable engagements! Plus, after your voyage, a champagne breakfast for two awaits you at the **Napa General Store**.

Since you have woken up so early today, I have arranged the rest of the day for some early wine tasting to conclude by mid-afternoon, giving you ample time for a relaxing wine country siesta. This way, you will be refreshed enough to enjoy an evening out on the town. *D'accord*?

There are only two ways up and down the Valley, Hwy 29 and the Silverado Trail. Both are scenic drives which allow you to stop at numerous wineries along the way. After your champagne breakfast, hop on Hwy 29 to head up the Valley. I would suggest stopping at two of my favorite wineries in Rutherford. First stop, **St. Supery Winery**, which offers wine education, shopping and a variety of lovely wines. Check in advance for their "Blending Seminar," a fantastic opportunity to learn about wine varietals, experience a tutored tasting, and blend your own bottle of wine to take home.

A little further down Hwy 29, stop at **Milat Winery** to taste some amazing wines (Chenin Blanc is my favorite) produced by the Milat family and sold exclusively on-site. They are a fun, personable family who take great pride in their Napa heritage.

Continue driving through the Valley, passing Yountville, Oakville, Rutherford, then driving through St. Helena to cross over Deer Park Road to Silverado Trail. Now start heading back to Napa, unless of course you want to see our last town in the Valley, Calistoga, where you can also easily cross through to Silverado Trail later on. Depending on traffic, it could take thirty to forty-five minutes from Napa to Calistoga. Make advance reservation for "Appellations & Appetizers" at **Pine Ridge Winery**, where Chef Eric Maczko pairs dishes to wines from this small production winery, a fun and tantalizing way to end your day.

Once back on Silverado Trail, if you are up for dining out, the most romantic restaurant in the area is **Bay Leaf.** Surrounded by a lush rose garden, this enchanting estate produces delicious food and a very romantic atmosphere. Otherwise, one could always opt for room service after such a long day.

SUNDAY

Sunday is the day to truly take advantage of your shared Golf & Spa package. Arrange your early tee ahead of time, and select and schedule your pampering spa treatments. As I mentioned before, this itinerary works well for a sociable group of couples. Both the men and women in the group have a chance to revel in some gender-friendly bonding time if desired, and each couple will still have plenty of relaxing hours à deux – a perfectly luxurious balance of socializing and intimacy.

After concluding your fabulous R&R and packing for the journey home, make one final stop out of town for a proper wine country send off. Pop a bottle of sparkling on the Chateau's impressive patio at **Domaine Carneros** to say good-bye. A classic French-style chateau located in the Carneros appellation of South Napa, this winery is amazingly picturesque, a perfect place to bid *adieu* to Napa Valley...

ehefritsch.com

HARVEST INN

ENDLESS ROMANCE

FRIDAY
ACCOMMODATION | HARVEST INN

Hidden behind vivid green topiary, sequoias, and lush gardens, Harvest Inn welcomes you with elegant red brick walkways around the beautiful grounds. Choose from an array of romantic packages, not forgetting the Elopement Package for those hoping to tie the knot. After you check in, curl up in front of the great room's cobblestone fireplace, and start your wine tasting weekend off right with the Inn's complimentary Friday and Saturday night tastings poured by local wineries.

After unwinding, prepare for a wonderful dinner at **Tra Vigne** in St. Helena. This Italian restaurant hosts a romantic atmosphere, upscale service and delicious food. Choose between eating outside on the Tuscan-inspired patio or inside the bravura dining area with high-ceilings, elegant décor, and a hand carved bar. The mouth-watering dishes are sure to tantalize, but I suspect that the classically romantic feeling of Tra Vigne will influence more than just your taste buds.

TRA VIGNE

SATURDAY

Embarking from the heart of the Valley is the ideal way to start a day of vino and amour. Begin with some planned wine tasting tours, such as the one offered by **Sterling Vineyards**, "(o)ne of the more spectacular wineries in Napa Valley," according to Frank Prial of *The New York Times*. The reserve tour and tasting at 11 a.m. starts with a tram ride up the hill to the winery, where you will gasp at a nearly 360° aerial view of the valley. Your experience at Sterling will also include vintage wine tasting and an escorted winery tour led by an experienced guide.

Across the street from Sterling Vineyards is another whimsical winery, **Clos Pegase Winery**, "where vine meets divine." This charming place offers an array of visual and palatable pleasures for any couple. In accordance with Greek mythology, Pegase represents the marriage of wine and art, which is exactly what you will discover here. A fascinating blend of modern and classical art pieces shrouds the property, including a "temple to wine and art" by architect Michael Graves. Along with its amazing artistic treasures, Clos Pegase also boasts special caves where the vineyard's sophisticated wines undergo the aging process, and welcoming, convenient picnic facilities.

On weekends, every half hour, there is a tasting tour at a breathtaking new winery, **Castello di Amorosa**. Allow yourself to be guided through this Italian-inspired castle to explore the stairway-filled towers, a medieval torture chamber, vast wine cellars, and Italian artisan hand-painted murals, "where no detail was overlooked," says *The Boston Globe*. If you have never had the pleasure of exploring ancient European castles, this is your chance to explore an accurately replicated version crafted entirely from select materials imported from Italy. The result has every ounce of character inherent to an authentic Italian castello.

To continue the theme of vino and amour through dinner, there is no better restaurant than the **Martini House**. Romance is inherent to this place, whether you're curled up beside the cellar's hidden fireplace or lounging under the twinkling lights of the fig trees in the garden. This fine dining establishment is the perfect place to dress up and indulge yourselves in a special wine country evening.

After dinner, stroll down St. Helena's Main Street before heading back to the hotel. If you're in the mood for a nightcap, stop at **Ana's Cantina**, one of the only local watering holes open late, for some live music and a margarita.

SUNDAY
Put on your hiking shoes, grab your bottled water and drive to Mount St. Helena to start your hike to the top. The mountain is absolutely beautiful, and was even chosen for Robert Louis Stevenson's honeymoon with his wife, Fanny. The place is also thought to be the inspiration for Spyglass Hill in Stevenson's book *Treasure Island*. Take in the evergreen Californian landscape on the trail upwards. Once at the top on a clear day, you can view the San Pablo Bay. The sweeping panoramic views are memories to be treasured together.

After you have worked up a sweat, treat yourself to a dip in Calistoga's natural hot mineral springs. Purchase a day pass at **Calistoga Spa Hot Springs** and soak the rest of the morning away in one of their four mineral pools.

Afterwards, savor lunch at **Rutherford Grill**, a local favorite, located on Hwy 29 in Rutherford. They don't take reservations, so be prepared for a worthwhile wait. Everything on the menu is fantastic, including a great wine and cocktail list. Plus, they have an outside bar to help quench your thirst while you wait for your table.

End your day with a final tasting at **Elizabeth Spencer Wines**, located directly across the street from Rutherford Grill. Here you will be able to make any last wine purchases of varietals sold exclusively in Napa Valley. Don't go home thirsty and empty handed – bring a little Napa sunshine with you!

REDD

2005

NAPA VALLEY

RED WINE

Chapter four

THE LANGUAGE OF WINE

WINE TASTING 101

ADVICE FROM LOCAL WINE DIRECTOR, CHRIS BLANCHARD

THE LANGUAGE OF WINE

WINE TASTING 101

*P*arlez-vous le vin? Chris Blanchard, Master Sommelier, and Wine Director at REDD, generously translates the language of wine for its uninitiated followers. In the following Q & A, he demystifies the potential for pretense surrounding the world of wine, allowing anyone visiting Napa Valley to feel confident during their wine tasting adventures. With a down-to-earth approach, he shares the basics about wine, its pairing with food, purchasing a celebrated bottle, and why this ancient beverage has become so popular in recent years.

Once a shoe salesmen, Chris completely transformed his career, becoming one of the most sought-after wine educators. His sinful humor and humble attitude toward the subject of wine have brought him great popularity and respect in the Valley. Chris is extremely knowledgeable in his pairings of wine and food, and his efforts to educate wait staff and inspire the public to start their own love affair with wine are sincere and effective. As he says: "It doesn't have to be complicated. You should just drink what you enjoy."

When Chris isn't teaching, tasting, and continuing his own education by tasting at local wineries weekly, he is an aspiring DJ who enjoys spending his downtime with friends at Napa Bowl. Far from the sophistication of REDD, local dives make Chris feel at home, and he hopes (as I do) that the misconception of wine as innately pretentious and inaccessible becomes as passé as White Zinfandel.

CHRIS BLANCHARD
Wine Director at REDD

jaimefritsch.com

CASTELLO DI AMOROSA

COMMON SCENTS & TASTE TO KEEP IN MIND

CHARDONNAY: medium to fuller-bodied, rich in style, often oaky. Think of warm buttered toast just out of your oven. Especially in Napa, you will get a lot of baked apple, roasted pear, yellow fig. Sometimes you can get tropical flavors too, such as papaya or melon, depending on the wine.

SAUVIGNON BLANC: Fresh lawn clippings, grapefruit, citrus, orange peel. More fragrant scents, such as gardenia and honeysuckle, and lighter-bodied than Chardonnay.

CABERNET SAUVIGNON: Cedar, roasted red bell pepper, blackberry, black currants, and tobacco. Robust and full-bodied.

PINOT NOIR: cherry, raspberry, mushroom characteristics, country road after a rain, damp. Medium to full-bodied.

MERLOT: cherry pie, raspberry, chocolate, mocha, espresso beans. Medium-bodied.

ZINFANDEL: strawberry jam, raspberry, blueberries, rich and syrupy, tannins are lighter, high alcohol content. Full-bodied.

WINE EDUCATION

Q Part of your job entails educating people about wine. What are the three most important things to know?

A The most important thing to know about wine is, firstly, what the varietals (grapes) are. Secondly, where is the wine from, and thirdly, who made the wine? For example, when we ask who makes the wine it can be the same grape from the same soil, but the winemaker's style dictates the final product. There is a region in France where two neighbors can have the same grapes from the same soil, but because of their style of producing wine, they are two very different wines.

Q Can you share with us the most common white & red varietals that you would find in California?

A Every winery makes a Chardonnay. Sauvignon Blancs are made here too, and then usually the wine makers will produce another wine that they enjoy making, such as a Viognier or Pinot Blanc. Certain regions are known for certain wines. Napa is known for Cabernet Sauvignon. Sonoma is known for Zinfandel; Zinfandel is the official grape of California.

Q Can you explain the language of wine? What is some common terminology?

A The best way to describe wine is in the description of the weight of the wine. Is the wine full bodied, heavy, or light? When I teach wine education to servers, I tell them to describe the weight of the wine with their guests. Sauvignon Blanc is a lighter-bodied wine, and it always has the same general flavors: pear, apples, grapefruit, lemon, lime. That's a good way to describe it. Also, talk about acidity. What's the acid level? When you take a lemon and bite into it, how tart is it? Most California and New World wines are going to have lower acidity because it's a warmer climate. So the cooler it is, the less ripe the grapes are going to get. The more ripe grapes get, the acidity goes down and the sugar goes up. That's another way to talk about wine and seem like an expert. All the winemakers want to emulate the Old World and have bright tasting, big fruit, balanced wine.

Q   What is the simplest way to describe a wine you like?

A   The most important to thing to think about when you taste wine is if it is balanced. Does it have too much oak? Is the fruit muted? If those things are all out of balance that won't change with time. If a wine is balanced initially, then it will continue to age that way. Just like a cocktail, if the bartender makes a drink that has the perfect blend of alcohol, lime juice, etc., then it is a great drink. You should think of wine the same way. Go ahead and describe it that way, too.

WINE TASTING ETIQUETTE

Q   There are five different ways to taste wine in Napa: barrel, walking tour, seated tasting, table service, and wine bar tasting. Which ones do you prefer and why?

A   If you have a lot of time, it would be best to sit down and have a winemaker talk to you about the wine. Some wineries, such as Franciscan, offer times to taste with someone leading you through to educate you about what they did with each wine. If you don't have time, you should just check out the list of what they are offering and ask to taste what you are most interested in. Don't taste everything – just pick the three you are the most interested in. Again, if you have time, barrel tasting is awesome for seeing how the wine is developing.

Q   Why are some wineries by appointment only? And is it better to have appointments?

A   Yeah, I think it's better to have an appointment. The reason why some of the wineries are by appointment only is because of zoning laws in Napa County. They don't want the roads to get crowded, and better quality wineries want to spend time with you as you taste their wine. Appointments usually are half an hour or more, and allow you to really get to know the wines and the winery. You should only do three wineries a day so you can talk to the people, and get to really know the story behind the wine.

Q Best advice for tasting in the Napa Valley? Biggest mistakes?

A The very best advice is to plan your days ahead of time. Make appointments ahead of time; if they don't do appointments, call and arrange a time to meet with someone, especially if it's your favorite wine. People love to share their knowledge with you and hear that you love their product. Again, stick to the three wineries a day, so you don't get stressed trying to see too many places. Biggest mistakes: make sure not to drink too much, because then you are not able to enjoy the next wine. Wine buyers and critics have to drink a lot during the day, but they spit their wine out, which I recommend. Tasting the wine still allows you to experience all its flavors, and swallowing it only allows you to get the effects of the alcohol. Basically, don't drink too much and plan your day!

jaimefritsch.com

CHRIS PAIRING WINE & FOOD,

Q What's the best way to swirl, taste, and talk about wine while at a winery?

A When you walk into the winery, to gain a little more respect, make sure to pick your wines. Swirl it around and spit, and maybe take some notes — that's how professionals do it. The relationship you build with the person at the bar is really important. Ask them what their favorites are or what they really like. Trust me, you will get the support that you need, and they will tailor your tasting especially to you.

WINE POPULARIZATION & PRICING

Q Each year, more and more visitors come to Napa Valley. Why has wine and wine tasting become so popular?

A I guess I would chalk it up to a couple of things: the press on wine, and the popularity of fine cuisine. More people are going out to eat; especially with the popularity of cooking shows and celebrity chefs, people really are more interested in dining out and learning about wine. The sophistication that wine offers people is appealing too. It has a better image than say, drinking beer. The movie Sideways made wine tasting more popular as well, not to mention the known health effects of drinking a little red wine everyday.

Q Why are some good wines $100 and others $20?

A That's a question I get a lot of the time. If you try a wine that retails for 20 bucks and one that retails for 100, just because it's more expensive doesn't mean you have to give it more respect. I tell my Mom to try a $10 bottle and a $100 dollar bottle, and she always thinks the $100 one will taste better – but it doesn't always. There are a lot of nuances and complexities that go into a higher-priced wine. Also, there is the price of marketing, promotion of the brand, and price of the vineyard land. You also have scarcity, which leads to higher price and demand. There are a lot of expenses that need to be taken into consideration when looking at pricing. The bottom line is, if it's worth $100 dollars to you, then buy it. I love some wines that are $250, and they are worth it to me.

Q What are some of the reasons to buy from the winery where you are tasting?

A Don't feel that because you're at the winery, you have to buy the wine; if you don't like it, don't buy it. However, if you really like something, go for it, especially if you can only get it at the winery. Buy some extra bottles to have as keepsakes too.

WINE & FOOD PAIRING

Q Many wineries are now offering wine & food pairing. Can you explain why?

A I think the wineries want to be different, and again there is the huge popularity of celebrity chefs and food culture. Wine can change so much with food, so winemakers can really show the value of their wine by paring it with certain dishes. If they have a really nice Pinot Noir, perhaps it's nice on its own; but pair it with a mushroom tart and some truffle oil, and they can get all different kinds of tastes and nuances out of the wine.

Good food and wine are great on their own, but when you combine them, it can add a new "superpower." The main components of food, say, a halibut dish, can be prepared a few ways, and you should look at that when pairing wine. If the dish is made with butter or herbs versus oil and tomatoes, the wine should pair properly – heavier wine for heavier food, and vice-versa. Scallops made with a creamy, rich sauce should be paired with a full-bodied wine to complement the dish. On the other hand, oysters are light-bodied and should be paired with a light wine. The rule of thumb is pairing the weight of the dish with a similar weight in wine.

Q What wines are hot right now?

A The hottest wine right now is Pinot Noir because of the movie *Sideways* and because of its affinity for food. Syrah is also very poised to do something soon. It's got the machismo of a Cabernet Sauvignon, peppery, meaty, gamey and delicious.

ROMANCE

Q What wine do you find the sexiest?

A Rosé sparkling wine, such as Schramsberg Reserve.

Q The Most Romantic?

A Merlot, because it's like a fuller-figured gal: silky, big fruit, and velvety.

Q Your pick for most romantic winery in Napa Valley, and why?

A Cain Vineyard and Winery is romantic because it's overlooking the valley. It's especially romantic when there is hanging fog over the valley. It has a rustic cabin feel, and offers a lot of privacy. Also Pride Mountain Vineyards, again really rustic and romantic. The last thing you want to do on a really romantic trip is to go to a very packed winery. Far Niente is very beautiful too, with the gardens, classic cars and gorgeous grounds. It makes you feel like you're in a different country.

WINE TERMINOLOGY

ACIDITY
When in perfect balance, acidity is what gives wine its fresh, crisp character; but like all sensuous equilibriums, this is a delicate one to achieve. Acid levels that are too high will render wine sharp and bitter, while too small an amount can leave a wine seeming "flat."

APPELLATION
Sometimes, it is about where you are; this is the term used to describe the region where a particular grape was grown and ripened to perfection.

AROMA
As in love, so in wine: when we talk about new love, we speak differently than we do about mature, time-tested love. In the same way, the terms used to describe a wine's scent depend upon its ripeness. "Aroma" refers to younger wines, while the more sophisticated "bouquet" is reserved for mature wines.

BARREL'S BALANCE
A harmonious relationship that must be struck between various elements of wine in order to produce delicious results. Acids, fruits, tannins, alcohol level, and other pieces come together in this balancing act.

BARREL
Sometimes called a cask, the traditionally wooden barrel provides a context in which the magic of fermentation occurs.

BODY
Beauty comes in every shape and size imaginable. Since we are highly sensitive and sensuous beings, the tiniest difference in weight imparted by a wine to our mouths will be noticeable, and called light, medium, or full-bodied.

BRIGHT
You will find that a wine with superior sparkle and clarity pleases almost as much as the light dancing in your lover's eyes.

DECANTING
This is the important process in which a decanter is used to separate undesired sediment from the wine, ensuring its prized "brightness."

DRY
Each to his or her own: those who prefer "dry" wines appreciate low levels of residual sugar, while others savor the intense sweetness. As if it isn't hard enough to figure out what floats your boat, a major exception to be aware of is sparkling wines — when they're referred to as "dry," it means they're sweet!

ESTATE WINERY
Farms are required to have a United States winery license in order to produce and sell their bounty on-site.

FINISH
Our senses linger in pleasurable states long after the event itself has passed; thus after wine is swallowed, its "finish" on your tongue will tell you a great deal about its quality.

FRUIT
These ones are not forbidden, thankfully. In fact, they are the main component of wine, and not restricted to grapes; a myriad of other fruits are employed to enhance the wine's character, such as pear, plum, cherry, blackberry, and many more.

LEGS
There's nothing like a great pair. After wine has been swirled in its glass, tell-tale tracks of liquid cling to the sides, betraying levels of alcohol and glycerol. Even though they're also called "tears," there's no need to mourn – unless of course your glass is empty.

NEW WORLD WINE
A whole new world of wine has come into being, hailing from places off the beaten path in Argentina, Australia, Canada, Chile, New Zealand, South Africa and United States. It pays to be adventurous…

NOSE
Whoever said wine doesn't have personality? Indeed, its aromatic "nose" will either beckon you to a taste, or repel you forever with its sharp odor.

OLD WORLD WINE
There is always great richness to be enjoyed from the fruits of tradition: the products of historical wine growing regions in Europe and North Africa have a reputation for a reason.

PALATE
Red or white, young or aged, New World or Old, every wine brings its own unique taste and feel to the table.

RESERVE
Once again, as in love, so in wine: sometimes we're lucky enough to stumble upon a bottle so superior to the others that we'd be nuts not to snatch it up and hold on for the ride. This term will let you know when you've found yourself a winner – in the wine department, that is.

Romantic Napa Valley

efritsch.com

Chapter five

ROMANTIC VIGNETTES

WINERIES

ARTESA WINERY

Artesa is a local secret, known as the "Jewel of Carneros." Located in the Carneros appellation, this stunning estate was designed to blend seamlessly into the natural landscape. To the naked (and especially vino-tinted) eye, it appears to emerge organically from the pristine Carneros hills, providing sensational views of Carneros and the San Pablo Bay — an ideal spot for the making of romantic memories.

As a complement to the winery's brilliant architecture, local artist Gordon Huether creates some fascinating contemporary pieces to further enliven your visual experience. Admired by figures such as Robert and Margrit Mondavi, Huether specializes in larger-scale designs using a variety of media, most often glass, metal, and canvas. Your first peek at his work will be the unique sculpture garden welcoming you onto the property. Cascading waters then follow you up the stairs to an entrance adorned by breathtaking fountains. "Creating art for exhibit at Artesa over the years has been an opportunity to experiment and explore my many diverse creative interests. The poetic balance of the beautifully crafted wine, extraordinary architecture and fine art truly makes Artesa an exceptional experience that I'm delighted to be a part of," says Huether. The winery's exhibit of his work changes constantly, so you will be treated to something new every time you visit.

Don't be fooled, though; your time at Artesa will not be remembered solely for the visual stimulation. Ecstasy of the palette materializes in varied forms here: perhaps you're in the mood for Vino con Queso, a Cheese & Wine Experience, which includes a guided tasting of their small production Limited Release and Reserve wines with Artisan cheeses. Viticultural enthusiasts should reserve their spots for a hands-on exploration through the Vines & Wines tasting tour of Artesa grapes right off the vine. Whatever your desire for the day, it will be met with more than you both could have imagined.

ARTESA
1345 Henry Road
Napa, CA 94559
707.224.1668
www.artesawinery.com

CASTELLO DI AMOROSA

Yes – a castle in the wine country! It took fourteen years and over thirty million dollars to finish, but Daryl Sattui has finally fulfilled his boyhood dream of building Castello di Amorosa, or "Castle of Love." In honor of his Italian heritage, Sattui has succeeded in replicating an authentic Italian castle complete with Italian-style courtyards, a traditional drawbridge, surrounding moat, chapel, torture dungeon and impeccable wine cellars. Italian artisans were brought in to create colorful frescos throughout the castle, ancient wooden doors were salvaged from a crumbling European castle, and a medieval stone fireplace was shipped straight from Italy, all to create an accurate replica and an unbelievable experience for its visitors.

Considered the biggest and most recent tourist attraction, tours through the castle are available by reservation only, allowing you a guided exploration of every fascinating corner and cranny. Imagine yourself wandering along pathways of imported Italian cobblestones, filled with excitement and wonder at being surrounded by a genuine Italian castle magically reincarnated here in the Napa Valley. Wind your way up its towers on spiraling staircases to arrive at breathtaking views of Calistoga.

"(A) spectacle…with eye-popping detail…Imitation was never so sincere," raves the *San Francisco Chronicle*. The wine you will discover here is equally impressive; in addition to the bright reds and alluring whites, Daryl Sattui also offers some extraordinary sweet wines, which are often hard to find in Napa Valley. His wines are exclusively sold on the premises, which is something to consider when making purchases in the Valley. Obtaining wines that you won't find anywhere else render them especially valuable treasures worthy of saving for a special occasion with your sweetheart.

CASTELLO DI AMOROSA
4045 Saint Helena Highway
Calistoga, CA 94515
707.942.8200
www.castellodiamorosa.com

At the foot of Mount St. Helena resides a world-class winery that takes serious winemaking to a revolutionary level – literally. Owned by vintner Jim Barrett, Chateau Montelena is as significant today as it was more than three decades ago, when the fruits of its firm philosophy, "Make the best, period," rocked the world, signaling a new era in superior winemaking.

At the legendary Paris Tasting of 1976, a precocious new generation of Californian wines famously outshone some of France's most historically-revered varieties. Intended to address the rising international buzz about surprising new wines being produced in California, this strictly-controlled blind tasting was conducted by an executive panel of world-renowned French experts. To France's great dismay, Napa Valley took the *gâteau*, and the frosting, too: Chateau Montelena's '73 Chardonnay defeated the French Meursault-Charmes '73, while Stag's Leap Wine Cellars '72 beat out the highly-prized Mouton-Rothschild '70. *Quelle surprise!*

Chateau Montelena remains grounded in a traditional beauty that honors its beginnings. Hidden behind the winery under layers of green ivy emerges a classic stone castle carved into the hillside, reminiscent of an old French chateau. More than a simple tourist attraction, it functions as a unique wine tasting facility and a serious winery calls for serious tastings, so make sure to experience the Library and Current Release Tastings, which feature some of the rarest and most highly sought California wines, period. Remarking on Chateau Montelena's Cabernets in his book, *The Great Wines of America*, expert Paul Lucaks says, "Over the years, this full-flavored Cabernet has come to serve as a benchmark for quality not only in Napa, but all across the winemaking world." From the castle, you will enjoy spectacular views of Jade Lake; envision floating white swans, Chinese gardens, and ornate gazebos perfect for a romantic outdoor lunch. Gaze in wonder at royal Mount St. Helena as you relax amid the weeping willows and feed crumbs to the passing swans, ducks, and turtles – and contemplate how you will ever possibly leave.

CHATEAU MONTELENA

1429 Tubbs Lane
Calistoga, CA 94515
707.942.5105
www.montelena.com

DARIOUSH

Inspired by the Persian culture and its famous sense of hospitality, this magnificent winery reflects Darioush Khaledi's lifelong dream of creating incredible wine in an aesthetically outstanding environment. His modern take on the sophisticated beauty of ancient Persepolis beckons you to indulge in a truly unique and unforgettable tasting experience.

Having grown up sneaking curious sips from the barrel in his native Shiraz, Khaledi always knew he was meant for winemaking. His intense passion for the industry are evidenced in the noble architecture and design of the 22,000-square-foot Darioush, which features gorgeous interior waterfalls, pools brimming with pink lotus flowers, and imagery that will transport you to another world from the moment you step on the property.

Khaledi's appreciation for the breathtaking and sensually satisfying reveals itself just as much in the meticulous processes undertaken to create the fabulous wines produced on his estate. In order to take full advantage of your time in this noble paradise, make sure to secure reservations in advance for the "Fine Wines, Artisan Cheeses" tour. This will allow you to savor Darioush's coveted limited release, special release and library wines in a private tasting, accompanied by an incredible array of delicious, small-production artisan cheeses from the highest quality family-owned farms in California, including cheeses from the highly popular Cowgirl Creamy. Nothing like a little nouveau-exotic decadence to get the romance under way!

DARIOUSH WINERY

4240 Silverado Trail
Napa, CA 94558
707.257.2345
www.darioush.com

DEL DOTTO VINEYARDS

I magine strolling through halls resounding with music from *The Phantom of the Opera*, looking up to observe Italian marble pillars, exquisitely hand-blown glass chandeliers, and vibrant frescos. The grandiose winery has a Cathedral feel to it, and in honor of Dave Del Dotto's Italian heritage, its décor is reminiscent of Classic Venetian architecture. Aspiring to be the "ultimate wine tasting experience in the world," this new winery is set to provide a mesmerizing journey for the five senses.

All tastings are by appointment only, including the popular Cave Tour, given daily, and Wine & Food Experience tasting, available on select days. While exploring the candlelit caves, you will enjoy an extensive barrel tasting in order to learn the characteristics of cave-aged wines and to savor their rich essence. Del Dotto declares that its cave tour is the finest for wine collectors in the world. I would add that it's an amazingly romantic tour for anyone who enjoys drinking wine!

Del Dotto's on-site chef, Joshua Schwartz, gathers inspiration from the vineyard's wines, taking the same approach to food as his former boss, Thomas Keller. He says that he "cooks from passion, with an understanding to be creative and different. The idea is to create memories with food." Each day, Joshua prepares high-quality dishes to complement the featured wines, such as Kobe Beef Sliders or Red Wine braised short ribs wrapped in chicken-fried steak. Along with an arrangement of assorted charcuterie, ripened cheese and pizzas for daily tasting, Joshua hopes to create an unforgettable memory for guests at Del Dotto.

DEL DOTTO VINEYARDS

1055 Atlas Peak Road
Napa, CA 94558

707.963.2134
www.deldottovineyards.com

DIAMOND OAKS WINERY

Nestled away in the tranquil foothills off Highway 29, Diamond Oaks transports you directly into a wine country state of mind. This is a family-owned estate whose motto, "patience is the key to excellence," demonstrates itself in the form of some truly marvelous wines.

The Maniar family takes pride in a twenty-year heritage of growing the best quality grapes for an array of prestigious wineries throughout Napa and Sonoma County. Having now taken up the task of producing their own wines using the highly-sought fruits of their labor, Diamond Oaks has produced some extraordinarily delicious results. Their strategy does indeed require patience; the grapes are grown in separate lots throughout the vineyard to provide the winemakers with a varied pool of tastes from which to select. Their award-winning 2005 Diamond Oaks Carneros Chardonnay attests to the value of such enduring patience.

The character of the winery itself is equally outstanding, featuring sweeping views of the Valley, rolling green hills, bountiful vineyards, and magnificent oak and olive trees scattered throughout. This is certainly a lovely environment for a peaceful and romantic picnic, whether you and your darling prefer walking the beautiful grounds in the sunshine, or dining on the cozy picnic tables under the shaded canopy of trees. Since you are likely to linger for hours as the sun goes down, don't forget to bring along your own Diamond Oaks treasure to accompany you – it would be a crime to go thirsty here!

DIAMOND OAKS
1595 Oakville Grade
Oakville, CA 94562
707.948.3000
www.diamond-oaks.com

DOMAINE CHANDON

Named Winery of the Year in 2005 by the California Travel Industry Association, Domaine Chandon offers stylish wine tasting that goes way beyond routine sipping and spitting. In a modern design, complete with a sophisticated tasting room and comfortable adjoining patio seating, the winery offers a variety of tastings: Prestige Cuvée, Classic, Varietal, and Reserve. Most well-known for their irresistible sparkling wine, Domaine also offers delicious still wines. Whether part of an entourage of couples or by yourselves, feel free to order a bottle of their sparkling wine at your table instead of tasting, and don't forget to sample some small bites from the sumptuous menu; you will no doubt find it difficult to move on to the next winery!

Tucked away next to the Veterans Home in Yountville and surrounded by beautiful gardens, fountain ponds, and artwork that "highlights exceptional local artists in unexpected ways," it's easy to figure out why the place is so popular. Check out their website for some sparkling wine cocktail recipes, wine & food pairing suggestions, and menu recipes to recreate your winery experience for friends and family back home, becoming their version of a "Savvy Entertainer."

Domaine Chandon boasts a proud history of being the first French-owned sparkling wine venture in the United States. They were also the first to bring four-star dining to Napa Valley in 1977. Étoile, the four-star restaurant on-site, is the only recognized fine-dining establishment at any winery in the Valley. According to Michael Bauer of the *San Francisco Chronicle*, "Domaine Chandon remains one of the most romantic special-occasion places in the valley." Innovative food, modern décor, and sophisticated service set this winery and its restaurant apart from the rest.

DOMAINE CHANDON WINERY

1 California Drive
Yountville, CA 94599

707.944.2892
www.chandon.com

ELIZABETH SPENCER WINES

J*'adore* Elizabeth Spencer wines! A husband and wife team, Elizabeth Pressler and Spencer Graham have always shared a passion for wine, and in 1998 they founded Elizabeth Spencer Wines. Both have many years of experience in the food and wine industry. They both assert, "We did not make our fortune in another walk of life and come here to fulfill our dream. This always was our life, and we've been blessed to live our dream." The winery was founded upon a love of food, wine, and each other, and that sense of love overflows into the creation of their wines as well.

Their tasting room is open to the public and located in the newly restored Rutherford Post Office brick building, originally built in 1872. This quaint and charming space is extremely welcoming, allowing you to become quick friends with your hosts and tasting neighbors; oftentimes when tasting here, I end up leaving with newly-made friends an added bonus to the amazing wine they offer.

As I am not a personal fan of strong oak flavor in wine, my favorite Elizabeth Spencer wines are made in stainless steel barrels. I'm told this technique makes the wine "crisp" with a "round palate." My favorites are the Sauvignon Blanc, Chenin Blanc, and Rosé of Pinot Noir. Become a club member to enjoy their wines year-round, as well as fringe benefits like a tasting in the garden, and a private tasting with Elizabeth and Spencer. An additional convenience is the close proximity to one of the best restaurants in the Valley, Rutherford Grill, which awaits you just across the street!

ELIZABETH SPENCER
1165 Rutherford Road
Rutherford, CA 94573
707.963.6067
www.elizabethspencerwines.com

FAR NIENTE

Far Niente translates roughly into "it's sweet doing nothing," which is exactly the light-hearted, carefree sentiment evoked throughout this very special winery. The Italian tradition of doing one's best to live *la dolce vita* was first transplanted here in 1885 with Far Niente's original construction. Now registered as a Historical Landmark, the winery was originally owned by a gold miner, and later reinvigorated in 1979 by Gil and Beth Nickel. In addition to his love for great wine, Gil brought with him family knowledge of fantastic gardening techniques and a background in classic auto racing. These varying interests shine through the surface of the winery in subtle and complementary ways: Far Niente houses an impressive auto collection, a stunningly designed landscape, half-mile-long wine caves, and luxury wines, specifically Chardonnay and Cabernet Sauvignon. With assistance from his partners, Dirk Hampson and Larry Maguire, as well as the Nickel family, Gil has successfully translated these passions into one of the best wineries around.

As you step into the stunning main building for your reserved guided tour, don't be surprised to find your name listed on the welcoming board, and to be greeted by the personable, attentive and humorous staff. The car collection is a must-see for many visitors, featuring rarities such as the 1966 Ferrari 500 Superfast, a 1961 Corvette Roadster and a 1951 Ferrari 340 America. As you stroll through the plush outdoor walkways, witness the largest collection of azaleas in the state!

Far Niente spares no expense in the interest of creating the most delicious and pleasurable experience possible, and is therefore considered somewhat expensive. However, I guarantee that it is worth every cent – take a bottle home to make the *dolce* memories last. Nickel & Nickel and Dolce are sister wineries; fun fact: Dolce is literally the smallest winery in the Valley, employing only one person! Their dessert wines are contained in 22-karat gold-designed bottles, and are liquid gold for any sweet wine lover. As you taste these amazing creations in the warm main room, nibble on the lovely cheeses and enjoy the alluring vista. There is no better way to relax together and let go of your cares than by visiting this haven of the sweet life!

FAR NIENTE WINERY

1350 Acacia Drive
P.O. Box 327
Oakville, CA 94562
707.944.2861
www.farniente.com

Start your adventure with a beautiful drive into the Mayacamas Mountains outlining the Western side of the Napa Valley, coming to rest on the lovely slopes of Mount Veeder. Tucked away next to the Christian Brothers Mont La Salle Institute and on the site of a former botanical garden is the renovated 1903 stone winery where The Hess Collection now stands in all its understated grace. Here, Donald Hess has successfully combined his appreciation for modern art and mountain wines to define the complete Hess Collection Experience.

For the past 45 years, Hess has been collecting contemporary works representative of a multinational variety of artists united by "vivid, powerful and thought-provoking" ideas and imagery. He tends to choose artists who are lesser-known, and strives to learn what drives the production of their individual works in order to share it with his mesmerized visitors. Impassioned as much in his art collecting as he is in his winemaking, Hess develops life-long relationships with these artists, supporting them and exposing their unique efforts to the public toward pragmatic ends rather than monetary ones. Many have gone on to become recognized and successful members of the visual arts community, including Anselm Keifer, Andy Goldsworthy and Francis Bacon.

True to his endeavor to reflect the places where the creation of art and the creation of wine intersect, The Hess Collection offers a Food and Wine Pairing Tour for the Palate by reservation. This tour begins with a guided walk through of Donald Hess' remarkable personal art collection followed by Chef Chad Hendrickson's wonderful and informative tasting of three wines and culinary dishes. Open daily to the public, you may also enjoy The Hess Collection's eminently drinkable wines at the beautiful cherry and wenge wood bar located in the property's historic stone distillery. Next, you can wander freely into the property's lovely garden to admire the reflecting pool and unique sculptures adorning it. By the time you conclude your foray into the Hess Experience, you will find yourselves looking at one other and the world with new eyes.

HESS COLLECTION
4411 Redwood Road
Napa, CA 94558
707.255.1144
707.265.3489 *for tour reservations*
www.hesscollection.com

KULETO ESTATE

Nestled in the mountains of the Hennessey Basin overlooking Napa Valley, and far away from the hustle and bustle of the two major wine tasting trails, Kuleto remains a precious and tranquil experience to share with your loved one. Owned by famed restaurateur Pat Kuleto (Jardinière, Martini House), this place evokes the rustic yet refined beauty of the Tuscan countryside, down to the smallest, hand-crafted detail. Come here to experience the culmination of Pat's quintessentially European philosophy of a rewarding life spent close to and in harmony with nature.

Upon your arrival on this magnificent property, you will be welcomed by Pat's two adorable and affectionate dogs, followed by the winery's warm and knowledgeable staff. The estate has been designed to incorporate Pat's own gorgeous Tuscan-style home, Villa Cucina, along with the attractive ranch and ninety-acre vineyard. Surrounded by hundred-year-old olive trees and glorious hillsides bearing painstakingly-nurtured vines, Kuleto makes for a perfectly relaxing and romantic refuge for travelers seeking the good life.

Make a reservation in advance for a personal walking tour of the property, which includes artisan cheeses and dried fruits picked by on-site chef Janelle Weaver to pair with the wines. With your own world-class Kuleto wine in hand, admire the view of sparkling Lake Hennessey and the valley below; gaze in wonder at the rolling green hills overflowing with coveted hillside-grown vines; explore the simple, understated architectural beauty of the Kuleto ranch, including gardens and landscapes dappled with grazing farm animals; and don't forget the magical Villa Cucina, which will have you dreaming of your own Tuscan hideaway. Afterwards, relax together on the comfortable patio seating, breathing in the soft, fresh air of the countryside – *deliziosa*!

KULETO ESTATE WINERY

2470 Sage Canyon Road
St Helena, CA 94574
707.963.2076
www.kuletoestate.com

Mumm Napa is one of my favorite wineries to lounge at on a sunny Sunday afternoon. Sipping my favorite sparkling wine, Cuvée M Red, and enjoying the vineyard views with the people I love (including my dear doggie) brings a contented smile to my face. Bring your friends and reserve a patio table in advance to ensure the best possible seating. Even sitting inside allows you to enjoy the beautiful views through a glass-enclosed tasting room. You will be treated to a lovely sparkling wine flight, composed of three divine glasses, paired accordingly.

Wine Enthusiast Magazine calls Mumm Napa "one of the best tasting experiences in America." Focusing exclusively on Sparkling Wines, Mumm's wines have recently scored 90+ points from top wine publications *Wine Enthusiast* and *Wine Spectator*. Master musician and Napa Valley fan, Carlos Santana, has collaborated with Mumm Napa winemakers Ludovic Dervin and Rob McNeill to create Santana DVX, an exclusive sparkling wine that will make a groupie out of you with its floral notes and creamy tones. Partnerships between established wineries and "celebrity winemakers" is a recent phenomenon in the Valley; other participants include Vince Neil, Jeff Gordon and Joe and Jennifer Montana.

A great new resource for couples on Mumm Napa's website is a wedding planner tool for couples to review quantity guidelines, food and wine pairing, and tasting notes. Whether going as a couple or not, make sure to visit the website to download and print the tasting notes to utilize during your own tasting, and prepare to marvel at all the new aromas and palates you will discover. It is a great way to build your wine education and develop your tasting skills; before you know it, you will become a sophisticated wine expert in your own right!

MUMM NAPA

8445 Silverado Trail
Rutherford, CA 94573

707.967.7700
www.mummnapa.com

the Holidays

90 Points Plus!

Blanc de Blancs 2001
Reserve Brut
DVX 2000

In Gold Holiday Gift Box

jaimefritsch.com

Romance of the Heart

NAPÁ VALLEY

2003

flirtation

NAPA VALLEY

2006

REFLECTION
late harvest cuvée

NAPA VALLEY

2005

jaimefritsch.com

O'BRIEN ESTATE

Seduction, Attraction and Flirtation: these are the names given to the wonderful wines Bart O'Brien and his beautiful wife Barbie handcraft at their family-owned winery. If you are seeking romance, this winemaking couple and the environment they have created form the quintessential example. On their third date to Napa, Barbie expressed a desire to move to the wine country and start her own winery. Bart, a storyteller and self-described "hopeless romantic," said that if that was her dream, then it was his dream as well. Hence the O'Brien Family Vineyard!

This appointment-only winery is located on the couple's beautiful property, next to their home at the foot of Mount Veeder. They focus solely on developing a romantic brand of wine, and enjoy customizing especially intimate visits for couples. Do not be surprised to hear the soft crooning of Billy Joel coming from the house – the O'Briens apply many personal touches, including special wine tastings guided by them. They even offer the "Romance Tour," which provides you and your sweetheart with absolute privacy, vineyards perfect for easy strolls together, a cozy picnic lunch for two, and wines that will leave you both starry-eyed.

Unlike the usual boring, ho-hum wine descriptions you will often find, Bart and Barbie spice up their wine labels. You might find yourself perking up to hear Barbie's description of her wine Flirtation: "Our dry rosé of merlot reveals alluring aromas of strawberries and crème, bright teasing acidity, a silky lingering finish and just enough grape skin contact to make it blush." Like a romance novel in a bottle, O'Brien wines will awaken and excite all your senses. Make sure to check out the Seduction Gift Boxes and join their Wine Lovers Club, so that you can continue the delicious affair even after you have parted ways with this truly lovely winery.

O'BRIEN ESTATE WINERY

1200 Orchard Avenue
Napa, CA 94558
707.252.8463
www.obrienestate.com

ROUND POND

Appropriately named after the place where founder Bob MacDonnell spent the most treasured and carefree moments of his youth, Round Pond is "a seamless blend of Old World traditions and state-of-the-art innovation." Located in the Rutherford area, most known for its superior Cabernet Sauvignons, this estate sets itself apart by producing not only the finest hand-crafted wines, but also the highest-quality red wine vinegars and fresh olive oil from its very own mill. In addition, everything is grown organically and produced using environmentally sustainable methods — evidence of the MacDonnell family's reverence for nature and its delicious bounty.

Round Pond's design provides an exceptionally seductive setting, no matter what time of year you care to visit. In summer, taste and relax on the lovely raised patio overlooking seemingly endless vineyards, from which only a small selection of grapes are chosen to produce prize-winning wines, such as Round Pond's 2004 Cabernet Sauvignon. In winter, cuddle together beside the blazing outdoor fireplace to savor the same wonderful view, delightful atmosphere, and extraordinary tasting pleasure.

A colorful array of tastings are yours for the choosing, so I present you with my three favorites. Firstly, the Wine and Food Pairing route teaches you Round Pond's secrets to creating voluptuous wines, accompanied by tantalizing *tapas*. Secondly, the romantic Twilight Tasting and Dinner begins with a tour of the winery and ends with a decadent multi-course feast composed of seasonal specialties. The third tasting I highly recommend will entertain your taste buds in more ways that you thought possible! The Al Fresco Lunch, "a perfect combination of fresh air and fresh foods," includes an in-depth tour of the estate olive mill and a guided tasting of the red wine vinegars and delicious olive oils created on-site (I personally love the blood orange and Meyer lemon-infused varieties). The tasting concludes with a leisurely family-style lunch featuring local artisan cheeses, breads, and meats, as well as seasonal fruits and vegetables. You and your sweetie will swear this is the ultimate outdoor culinary experience!

ROUND POND

886 Rutherford Road
Rutherford, California 94573
888.302.2575 & 707.302.2575
www.roundpond.com

RUTHERFORD HILL WINERY

Rutherford Hill Winery enjoys the distinction of having helped pioneer the creation of California Merlot decades ago, before it became such a hit among the masses. Its founders chose this particular site due to its environmental similarity to Pomerol, the famous Merlot grape-growing region in Bordeaux. Over the years, Rutherford Hill has expanded significantly in reputation, demand, and production rates. However, the Terlato family continues its dedication to constant improvement in standards of quality over quantity. Their time-tested process of production culminates in sprawling, mile-long caves in which 8,000 French oak barrels bring wines to an aged perfection. These caves are an attraction in themselves, as you'll be able to enjoy a romantic lunch or dinner inside them if you so choose.

This is the perfect spot for enjoying the outdoor patio and breathtaking views without missing a beat – or a taste. There is also an unparalleled variety of picnicking options, each of which offers a unique appeal. The Live Oak Grove is well-shaded and equipped for larger groups of people, while the one hundred-year-old Olive Grove is more intimate and romantic for couples and small groups, providing individual tables and a lovely gazebo. The private Upper Grove is located slightly above the winery and is thus pleasantly removed from the visiting crowd. Of course, all three groves offer spectacular views of the Napa Valley, as well as an array of convenient catering and barbecuing options offered by the winery.

Another element which makes Rutherford Hill special is a unique opportunity to play "winemaker for the day." The creative and educational "Blend-Your-Own-Merlot" tasting tour takes you on a fully guided tour of the grounds and caves, tasting from the barrels to notice the different stages of aging – but it doesn't end there. You are now given free reign to blend your own personal bottle of Merlot, selecting the varieties and flavors you enjoy most. The best part is you get to take a bottle of your own creation home with you, and enjoy the fruits of your labor long after departing from this memorable place.

RUTHERFORD HILL WINERY

200 Rutherford Hill Road
Rutherford, CA 94573
707.963.1871
www.rutherfordhill.com

SIGNORELLO VINEYARDS

'Twill make old women young and fresh,
Create new motions of the flesh.
And cause them long for you know what,
If they but taste of chocolate.

— James Wadsworth

Chocolate has long been considered a powerful aphrodisiac, thus a graceful marriage of chocolate and wine are an absolute must for a truly passionate weekend. The staff at Signorello Vineyards are experts in this regard. Make sure to schedule your Cioccolato & Wine Pairing Private Tasting ahead of time, and prepare for a wonderful composition of dark chocolates from Woodhouse Chocolates in St. Helena, California, specifically paired with an array of Signorello Vineyard wines. Nothing beats this awe-inspiring experience, especially with the Napa Valley sunshine overhead and your lover by your side.

Signorello Vineyards was established by Ray Signorello, Sr. and his wife Hope, who knew a thing or two about the pursuit of romance. The Signorellos say that what brought them to Napa Valley in the 1970's "was the romantic side of winemaking: growing grapes, working the land, and enjoying the wine country lifestyle of camaraderie, great wine and great meals." Ray Signorello, Jr. now carries on this dream and dedicates his life to the passion of winemaking, pairing the estate wines with quality cuisine. He also likes to share this passion with others by posting his personal wine tasting notes on the website for all to see and learn from.

Your private tasting at Signorello Vineyards is set on a Mediterranean-style patio with an infinity edge pool, lovely Italian statues and soothing water fountains. Closed off from the public, it overlooks the pristine Cabernet Sauvignon vineyards below and has a charming view of the valley floor. Even though you are close to the scenic Silverado Trail, you feel an ocean away from the humdrum of everyday life.

SIGNORELLO VINEYARDS

4500 Silverado Trail
Napa, CA 94558

707.255.5990
www.signorellovineyards.com

SILVERADO VINEYARDS

Set upon a knoll overlooking Stags Leap, Silverado Vineyards boasts one of the best panoramic views in the Valley. An open courtyard welcomes you to this Mediterranean-themed winery where you feel instantly at ease. Start in the oversized tasting salon, and slowly float between the tasting bar and the beautiful cobblestone terrace. Enjoy their Daily tasting, Library tasting or Saddleback Vineyard tasting of luscious Silverado wines.

Robert Louis Stevenson's book, *The Silverado Squatters,* profiles his 1880 stay in Napa Valley and his awe of the winemaking process; it was also the inspiration for the vineyard's name. "The beginning of vine planting is like the beginning of mining for the precious metals: the winegrower also 'prospects.'" Silverado Vineyards continues to handcraft wines that get consistently high ratings, particularly their Cabernet Sauvignon, Merlot and Sauvignon Blanc (the latter is my personal favorite).

If the process of winemaking intrigues you, or if you like relaxing in a lounge chair to enjoy the sweet vineyard air, then I'd recommend the Saddleback Vineyard Tour. It's a wonderful opportunity to learn more about what makes the Napa soil so special, among many other interesting wine facts. The small guided tour is described as an "intimate and educational" experience, where you walk into the winery's personal vineyards and start your training as resident winemaker for the day! This is a great way to learn more about wine, engage with wine professionals, and discover what is really going on behind the scenes as you gaze at the beautiful rows of vines – not to mention the amazing wines and delicious canapés that make this tour so worthwhile.

SILVERADO VINEYARDS
6121 Silverado Trail
Napa, CA 94558
707.257.1770
www.silveradovineyards.com

CALISTOGA RANCH

Chapter 6

ROMANTIC VIGNETTES

ACCOMMODATIONS

1801 FIRST LUXURY INN

Forget your past assumptions about traditional inns adorned with floral wallpaper, dried flowers, and run-of-the-mill antique furniture. Darcy Tunt, proprietor, has reinvented and redefined the modern Inn at 1801 First. From "period" Bed & Breakfasts to luxury boutique inns, Darcy insists on a supremely "unique and romantic experience for all her guests." Stylishly decorated with contemporary décor, Darcy has found a graceful way to combine the majestic feel of the property with a desirable contemporary appeal.

Built in 1903, there are many distinct nuances which set 1801 First apart from the many other charming B & B's in the historic downtown area. The luxurious amenities and attentive service include custom-made bedding, fireplaces in all of the rooms and an array of spa services offered in the privacy of your own room. Darcy's approach of unrestricted concierge service attracts many couples on a return basis. Also, the presence of a wonderful on-site chef kicks things up a notch. Unsurprisingly, 1801 First is consistently invited by *Condé Nast* for inclusion in the publication's "Recommended Hotels, Inns, Resorts, and Spas."

As Darcy herself can attest, "the Inn is all about romance." To take full advantage of this fact, try the "Romance Retreat Package." Spend two magical nights with your honey in one of the Inn's lovely rooms, complete with perfect places to curl up together by the fireplace to pop open that welcome bottle of champagne. You may also wish to request a luxurious Jacuzzi in the room, so that you may follow your complimentary one-hour couple's massage with a nice, long soak. The Inn aligns itself with some of the smaller family-run wineries nearby to heighten the level of personal attention you receive when you take the two free VIP wine tasting passes for the day. In addition, you will be treated to gourmet multi-course breakfasts, complimentary wine and hors d'oeuvres, and a free mini-bar always at your disposal. In essence, all your heart's desires can be filled here; so come relax and enjoy one another in the capable hands of 1801 First.

1801 FIRST LUXURY INN

1801 First Street
Napa, CA 94559
707.224.3739
www.1801first.com

AUBERGE DU SOLEIL

An unparalleled experience, this world-famous "Inn of the Sun" born of its award-winning restaurant is truly glorious to behold. The Auberge du Soleil offers intimate revitalization in a context of natural beauty and tasteful luxury unmatched elsewhere. Serenely perched in the hills overlooking Rutherford, this pioneering mecca of relaxation and romance in Napa Valley is a favorite of travelers, locals, and Hollywood celebrities alike. The resort's brilliant design was originally conceived by the legendary Michael Taylor, who helped prominent restaurateur Claude Rouas realize his dream here in 1985. The Auberge received instant acclaim for its seamlessly interwoven French Country *richesse* and fresh California flavor, rendering this the first luxury inn of Napa Valley.

Following its 20-year anniversary, the Auberge has undergone a new stage in its life, facilitated by Taylor's former protégé, Suzanne Tucker. Her updates are extremely mindful of her predecessor's vision, and have further increased the resort's capacity for providing the ultimate in sensual comfort and effortless romance. The soft tones and luxurious textures of Southern France are reincarnated in new forms, and the world-class Auberge Spa has been further expanded. A new chef brings with him delightful innovations to the famous Auberge Restaurant, and the renovated *La Plage* European-style pool area has guests raving.

Prepare to be enveloped by the lush Rutherford hillsides dotted with charming Provençale-style *maisons* full of rustic charm and every modern comfort imaginable. Glide through lovely French doors to your private terrace, where you will be treated to impeccable views of the valley. Venture out to La Pagode, the unbelievably romantic Japanese-style ryokan nestled amid fragrant vines and abundant olive groves; make sure to reserve it for couples spa treatments, private dinners, and warm-weather celebrations. Try the "Romance Package," which provides a two-night stay in a Garden View King Room, welcome wine and spa gifts, daily Auberge breakfasts, a four-course Auberge feast, and a 90-minute couples massage. Between the gorgeous accommodations, unbeatable cuisine, endless amenities and stunning natural beauty, you and your lover will wish for nothing more.

AUBERGE DU SOLEIL

180 Rutherford Hill Road
Rutherford, CA 94573
707.963.1211
www.aubergedusoleil.com

CALISTOGA RANCH

I f privacy and luxury are what you want, look no further: this secluded
hideaway offers couples serenity and harmony with nature. Tucked away on
former local camping grounds, Calistoga Ranch has designed 46 guest lodges
that blend perfectly into the expansive surrounding forest. As you step onto
your private wooden patio deck and breathe in the aroma of grand oak trees and
soft green pines swaying at your bedroom door, you will no doubt agree that
the architect's accomplishments are impressive. Affiliated with the renowned
Auberge Resorts, Calistoga Ranch is an exclusive four-star village-style resort that
provides a leisurely, sensuous backdrop for your romantic weekend *au naturel*.

Calistoga Ranch offers a variety of romantic packages conceived for your
mutual pleasure. I give you my top three: the "Starry Nights Package" offers
two nights in your own private lodge, a candlelit dinner at Calistoga Ranch's
Lakehouse Restaurant, a spa treatment for you both at the Bathhouse,and
a lovely bottle of wine and cheeses awaiting you by your own cozy fireplace
afterward. If you want to "Rekindle the Romance," you will receive a
dozen beautiful roses upon arrival, and enjoy three nights, a lovely candlelit
dinner for two, and breakfasts in bed. If you desire to "Expand Your
Senses" here, you will be treated to a romantic dinner at the Lakehouse
Restaurant, relaxing spa treatments, and even a winery tour. Don't forget the
tempting "Elopement Package," which can provide every desired detail for a
spontaneously romantic wedding.

The amenities and complementary activities are endless at Calistoga Ranch.
Most notably, the first-class Bathhouse spa offers a Jacuzzi with fireplace, a
fragrant eucalyptus steam room, and an array of splendid couples treatments.
Lounge in the steaming tub together as you watch the morning haze fade off
the mountain tops and glide over the pond. Renew yourselves in a yoga class,
take a swim in the heated pool, or enjoy everything from bocce ball and Ai
Chi to cooking classes and music concerts. My personal favorite is taking an
early-morning hike along the quiet, scenic guest-only trails to catch the dawn;
and feel free to bring your beloved pup along! Later on, sip those delicious
cocktails on the deck overlooking the picturesque pond. Promise each other
to return to this heavenly place of renewal again and again.

CALISTOGA RANCH

580 Lommel Road
Calistoga, CA 94515
707.254.2800
www.calistogaranch.com

With its relaxing natural atmosphere and attractive design, The Carneros Inn perfectly embodies the true nature of the Napa Valley countryside. A host of charming cottages and luxury suites make up this unique agri-chic destination, incorporating down-to-earth country views of green apple orchards, lush farmland, and vast vineyards with modern, sophisticated interiors for the romantic comfort you seek. Quietly situated in the Carneros appellation, The Carneros Inn was voted one of the "Top 25 Romantic Getaways in the World" by *Travel & Leisure Magazine*. It also scored a perfect 100% for its authentic setting and attentive service; so as they say, "Relax. You've found just the right place."

The country-modern allure of this luxury resort intermingles effortlessly with the rural landscape surrounding it. The inviting hilltop pool, first-class spa with indoor and outdoor treatments, and fitness and yoga studio provide convenient sources for indulgence and renewal without breaking the natural silhouette of the land. Three full-service restaurants await your *bon appétit:* The Hilltop Dining Room, Boon Fly Café and The Carneros Inn's signature establishment, affectionately known as FARM. Each place offers its own delights, but FARM is definitely my favorite for evening cocktails and a delicious dinner, while the Boon Fly Café is best for an eye-opening Sunday Brunch.

Seasonal packages vary throughout the year, but the most romantic is "Crush on You." With the discounted accommodation of your choice comes a warm welcome basket to start off your journey into relaxation with a bottle of hearty Cabernet and Charles' Chocolates raspberry heart truffles. You will also enjoy a romantic dinner for two at FARM, along with two fantastic spa treatments: the Virgin Coconut Scrub and Chocolate Massage make for a sinfully delicious package. From the staging to the setting, from the cuisine to the wine, The Carneros Inn is true luxury without pretense, and a welcoming host to love.

CARNEROS INN
4048 Sonoma Highway
Napa, CA 94559
707. 299.4900
www.thecarnerosinn.com

COTTAGE GROVE INN

*P*rovence, Tuscany, Vintner, Traveler... these are some names of the enchanting accommodations awaiting you at Cottage Grove Inn. As charming and whimsical as they sound, each cottage offers a unique, individually-themed appeal. The inviting town and world-famous mineral spas of Calistoga set the scene for your romantic stay. The theme of romance extends even to the ownership of the Inn itself: three lovely couples got together with the idea to spread the joy of romance by opening up the establishment in 1996. Since then, it has been calling to couples from near and far to take shelter. According to *Travel & Leisure*, "Calistoga has no shortage of cottage accommodations, but none are better-conceived than those at the new Cottage Grove Inn." Linnea Lundgren gave it a near-perfect rating in her *Best Places to Kiss in Northern California*, 5th Ed.

A short walk from downtown Calistoga, the Cottage Grove Inn allows you to explore the town together on foot. The charming historic downtown area offers many wonderful dining, spa, and shopping possibilities. Enjoy feeling like more of a local and less of a tourist as you return home from your exciting day to your own little Napa home-away-from-home. Under the protective cover of old elm trees, each of the 16 cottages feature old-fashioned whicker rocking chairs perfect for lounging on your own shaded patio. Enjoy the king-sized beds with cozy down comforters, custom-made furniture, private wood-burning fireplaces, luxurious robes, wet bar, and deep Jacuzzi bathtubs for two – all important ingredients for a luxuriously romantic weekend. The owners believe "creature comforts always enhance a relaxing getaway," so they have equipped each cottage with these valuable amenities.

Seasonal packages are available for couples, such as the Wintertime Cottage Spa and Winery Package, which includes a private cottage for two, your choice of 60-minute spa treatments, and a private wine tour and tasting at an exclusive local winery. Start off your stay with a customized gift basket from the Cottage Grove Inn's boutique shop prepared specially by the innkeepers for your special significant other. Also make sure to schedule a sensual couple's massage ahead of time -- as they say, it's all in the details, and this most certainly applies to the rules of romance.

COTTAGE GROVE INN

1711 Lincoln Avenue
Calistoga, CA 94515
707. 942.8400
www.cottagegrove.com

A stay at the Cottages of Napa Valley will fulfill your dreams of a tranquil sojourn in the countryside. The charming and colorful cottages are aligned in rows encircling the quaint historical property. The first cottage, built in 1929, was originally located on an orchard which hosted a local fruit stand. That same cottage (presently called #8) was used in 1939 for Clark Gable and Carole Lombard's romantic retreat while filming the classic "They Knew What They Wanted." Located on Darms Lane, which is actually named after my adopted grandmother's family, the property exudes an intriguing history. There was even a point where the cottages were rented to vineyard workers and returning WWII veterans. In 2004, the property was acquired by Mike Smith, and transformed into a present-day rustic and romantic retreat.

Surrounded by lush pines, sprawling fig trees, green lawns and multi-colored foliage, the Cottages of Napa Valley now offers modern comforts mixed with old-fashioned charms. *Wine Spectator* calls it "one of the most romantic and relaxed settings in Napa Valley." Each cottage is furnished with a king-sized bed under vaulted ceilings, a private kitchenette, a fireplace, and 2-person bathtub with heated bathroom tile floors. You are provided with comfy bathrobes and slippers, and access to your semi-private patio area complete with an outdoor wood-burning fireplace. For the adventurous, bicycle rentals are always available. The breakfast basket of pastries from Bouchon Bakery delivered to your front porch each morning will be a welcome wake-up call. Here, all the amenities one could desire in a romantic hideaway are right at your fingertips.

If tying the knot is in your future, reserve the entire property for a small intimate wedding; say your vows to one another under the lovely gazebo in the main garden. For a honeymoon site, look no further. A wonderful romance package for any couple includes two nights in your own special cottage, a bottle of chilled champagne upon arrival, a decadent dessert for two, a dozen fragrant roses, and an in-room couple's massage. Additional spa treatments can be added as well. Just imagine your lover's eyes sparkling with excitement as you walk through the door of your private cottage for the start of a fun, romantic weekend — truly priceless.

COTTAGES OF NAPA VALLEY

1012 Darms Lane
Napa, CA 94558
707.252.7810
www.napacottages.com

the cottages *of* napa valley

HARVEST INN

*"To sit in the shade on a fine day
and look upon verdure is the
most perfect refreshment."*

- Jane Austen

Enchantment starts to overtake you the very moment you arrive at the Harvest Inn. Surrounded by towering redwood trees and a feeling of natural serenity, you would never know that the Four Diamond retreat is located right off Highway 29. Delicately hidden behind soft green foliage amid a country-style landscape, this boutique hotel exudes genuine intimacy and effortless romance.

The charm of a country estate prevails throughout each of the 74 guestrooms and cottages, which often feature garden, fountain, and sun-kissed vineyard views. The various accommodations are scattered across eight acres of lush vegetation, where fruit trees, azalea bushes, and blooming tulips abound. The Inn also boasts a lovely Manor House with intricate architectural detailing, two outdoor swimming pools, fireside wine tasting, plush robes, wine country breakfasts, L'Occitane bath products and a wine bar, just to mention a few attractive amenities.

Surrender to the Harvest Inn's romantic package, and embark upon your own whimsical weekend in style. Begin with a deluxe guestroom for two complete with a king-size bed, a welcome bottle of champagne, and decadent chocolate truffles. Continue your journey into the land of amour with two spa treatments, either in your room or in the garden sanctuary, as well as a leisurely breakfast in bed and personal concierge services. The Harvest Inn also offers an elopement package and an assortment of wedding packages, such as "A Day to Remember" or "An Elegant Affair," depending on the specific wishes of each couple. With all that Harvest Inn has to offer, there is no doubt that a memorable experience awaits each and every heart who enters its doors!

HARVEST INN

1 Main Street
St Helena, CA 94574
707.963.9463
www.jdvhotels.com

MAISON FLEURIE

*I've dreamt in my life dreams that have stayed with me ever after, and changed
my ideas; they've gone through and through me, like wine through water,
and altered the color of my mind.*

~Emily Brontë

Dreamers, take note: Maison Fleurie, the aptly named "flowering
house," combines the simple elegance of Southern France with the
warm hospitality of wine country for an unbelievably romantic experience.
Considered an ideal haven for lovers, Maison Fleurie offers 13 quiet
guestrooms, each lovingly decorated and reminiscent of classic French
Country charm. This quaint bed and breakfast Inn succeeds in achieving an
exceptionally peaceful and personalized atmosphere. A member of the Four
Sisters extraordinary association of Inns, Maison Fleurie exemplifies what a
truly romantic hideaway should be.

The vine-covered brick construction of the Inn is over 130 years old. Three
main buildings make up the Inn's entirety, including a main parlor, the
carriage house and the old bakery building. Additionally, the property has
a comfortable hot tub, a pristine outdoor pool and incredibly colorful and
lush gardens overflowing with all the flowers you could ever wish for.
You will be treated to a delicious wine country breakfast each morning
and afternoon home-made treats, all passionately crafted by on-site chef
Sonia Torres, who lovingly caters to every guest's dietary needs and
personal temptations. Don't miss her scrumptious quiches and
delectable cheesecakes.

Take a chance with the "Isn't it Romantic" package, and invite romance in.
This popular offering includes a two night stay for two, a bottle of chilled
champagne, chocolate truffles, a fifty dollar voucher for dinner at Bouchon
or Hurley's (two of my recommended romantic restaurants), along with
Maison Fleurie's signature breakfast and afternoon delicacies. You might
also opt for the "On the Town" package, which includes all of the above
privileges for a one-night stay. Either way, *un séjour* at Maison Fleurie
guarantees happy dreams for any couple.

MAISON FLEURIE

6529 Yount Street
Yountville, CA 94599
800.788.0369
www.maisonfleurienapa.com

MERITAGE RESORT

The term "Meritage" was coined long ago by Napa Valley winemakers dedicated to producing wines that give the renowned French Bordeaux a run for its euros. The word combines "merit" and "heritage" to reflect deep reverence for successes of the past and excitement for future achievements beyond the tried and true. Practically speaking, it also serves as an identifier of wine that incorporates the best of several worlds, in which no grape variety overwhelms the other, working together harmoniously in a truly delicious and superior blend.

Celebrated as "the perfect blend for the perfect stay," the Meritage Resort is a wholly unique concoction expertly bottled into one flawless, remarkably self-contained resort. For starters, it boasts the only spa in the world located in an underground wine cave, its very own on-site wine tasting bar, the well-regarded Siena restaurant, and a gorgeous private chapel called Our Lady of the Grapes accompanied by a spacious Vineyard Terrace for the ceremony and reception of your dreams -- and that's just the beginning. Choose from an array of luxurious guestrooms and suites, enjoy yourselves in the extensive outdoor entertainment area, which includes a heated pool, bocce ball court, fire pit, and full poolside service, and relax with a great cocktail at the Meritage Bar. In truth, the many-flavored amenities offered at this resort rival all others, and are bound to tickle anyone's fancy.

The "Romance Package" offers a 2-night stay, a welcome bottle of sparkling wine and special "romance amenities," dinner for two at Siena, breakfast in bed every morning, take-home Spa Terra plush robes, and a 50-minute couples massage. The dramatically-designed, artisan-crafted Spa Terra is set within a magical, candlelit wine cave, and features steam grottos, waterfalls, and soaking pools. If that's not enough for you, go all-out for the "Jetting off to the Napa Valley" package, which provides private jet transport to the resort for up to 8 people, a 2-night stay in superior accommodations, private winery tours and barrel tasting, Siena breakfasts, and breathtaking hot air balloon rides! Come sample the exquisite craftsmanship and long-lasting finish of the Meritage blend, and take advantage of the fact that all the essential ingredients for a quintessentially romantic weekend have been crafted into a reserve blend just for you.

MERITAGE RESORT

875 Bordeaux Way
Napa, California 94558
707.251.1900   www.themeritageresort.com

NAPA RIVER INN

Situated downtown within the historic Napa Mill of 1884, Napa River Inn is a 66-room premiere luxury hotel and a member of the Historical Hotels of America. The Inn offers a romantic atmosphere of traditional Napa Valley elegance mixed with chic décor, resulting in a warm and welcoming feel for the many couples who frequent it. Overlooking the banks of the Napa River, the hotel occupies three buildings, named the Embarcadero, the Historic and the Plaza. You may also be interested to know that the Napa River Inn is famous not only for its rich history, but also for the Haunted House-style legends surrounding its past.

This fully-restored and authentically maintained waterfront hideaway is within close proximity to twelve tasting rooms, top-notch restaurants, fine art galleries, charming boutiques and colorful local nightlife. Even more conveniently, Napa Mill hosts an inclusive array of dining, shopping and entertainment establishments. Alan Shepp's mosaic fountain, "ARS LONGA VITA BREVIS" (Life is Brief But Art Endures) graces the property, depicting the "Triumphs and Tragedies" of the Napa Valley story, completing the historically educational theme. There is also a lovely waterfall, under which mosaic images of flora and fauna native to the Napa River have been installed.

Lovers are in for a treat with the Napa River Inn Romantic Getaway Package. Savor chocolate-covered strawberries and champagne waiting for you in your room. Sleep peacefully, and start your morning breakfast in bed with piping-hot treats from Sweetie Pies. Enjoy the pleasant views of Napa River from your comfy seat by the fireplace. This dog-friendly hotel warmly invites you to "hide away from the outside world," and relax in their capable hands. Take them up on an exciting bicycle getaway together, a honeymoon package, or a seductive spa package, along with a variety of other options to suit every couple's desires. In accordance with the rules of love, you also happen to be staying at a place consistently rated one of the best places to host a wedding. So come take a step back in time at this endlessly romantic Inn, and let your hopelessly romantic streak fly free.

NAPA RIVER INN

500 Main Street
Napa, CA 94559
707.251.8500
www.napariverinn.com

SILVERADO RESORT

Elegant and refined, Silverado Resort is a true reflection of wine country style and sophistication. The resort hosts a California Landmark Mansion, built in the 1870's, located in the heart of their facilities. The mansion has a long and colorful history – it is rumored to have been given as a wedding gift by General Vallejo to his daughter, and was named *Le Verge* after a previous owner's civil war battle; it has even hosted the likes of Theodore Roosevelt. Today it continues to stand as a handsome reminder of the Valley's noble past.

This truly classic resort includes a 16,000 square foot spa facility, seventeen plexipaved tennis courts, and a newly renovated main pool area. It also hosts competitive golf tournaments on the two pristine 18-hole, 360-acre golf courses designed by Robert Trent Jones, Jr., so staying active while on vacation won't be difficult here. In addition, you will be privy to two award-winning restaurants and a fun main lounge area where you can find cozy indoor fireplaces and delicious cocktails on the patio terrace. On weekends, even locals will join in on the good times, lending an authentic, connected feel to the place.

Being an expert in romance, Silverado Resort offers an array of attractive packages for couples. The popular "Romance Package" provides beautiful and spacious accommodations with lovely master bedrooms, a full kitchen and dining area, wood-burning fireplaces, and massages for two as well as a delicious breakfast. You may also go for a wine tasting trip to nearby Luna Vineyards, or opt for an in-room movie and a bottle of delicious champagne to compliment your perfect romantic evenings together at this utterly enjoyable resort.

SILVERADO RESORT
1600 Atlas Peak Road
Napa, CA 94558
707.257.0200
www.silveradoresort.com

SOLAGE

Solage is more than just a resort — it is a complete experience. This new, solar-powered, green-friendly hideaway is part of the Auberge Resorts, and it exceeds the expected level of luxury and high-end style associated with the name. Situated in beautiful Calistoga, just below Mount St. Helena, Napa Valley's dormant volcano, this modern California-chic establishment offers affordability and progressive opulence in the wine country. With 89 studio-design guestrooms to choose from, each rich with distinctly attractive style, every couple is certain to find true bliss at Solage.

This unique resort offers complimentary bike cruisers for all guests and staff to transport themselves around the resort. In line with their environmentally-conscious philosophy, Solage is also dedicated to serving organic and locally-grown produce. They are pet-friendly as well and even welcome your pampered pooch with a water bowl, a plush dog bed, and organic doggie treats! Start your stay with a refreshing splash in their stunning 130-foot swimming pool, then slip into a relaxing yoga class or play a round of bocce ball. Later on, sip cocktails at their hip Solbar, savor the modern Bistro "Sol-ful dining," and lounge around the cozy outdoor fire pits.

Solage is a strong promoter of health and wellness, so a trip to their impressive 20,000 square foot Solage Spa is a must. Indulge together in the natural geothermal spring waters, treat yourself to a pampering with Kate Somerville's skincare line, and pony up to the mud bar to relish in revitalizing volcanic goo. In an adventurous mood? Try a "Solage Mudslide for Two," their signature spa treatment, and relax completely with a couples massage afterwards. Choose Solage's seasonal "Winter Escape" package and snuggle together in the heated pools as the rain and fog glide overhead. Trust me, there's nothing more romantic, and you will both swear that you've found heaven on earth.

SOLAGE CALISTOGA

755 Silverado Trail
Calistoga, CA 94515
866.942.7442
www.solagecalistoga.com

VILLAGIO INN & SPA

Every couple should "escape to Tuscany" at this exquisite Four Diamond resort located in enchanting Yountville. The graceful ensemble of Italian cluster-style architecture, luxurious amenities and a tasteful, intimate atmosphere makes this Inn & Spa *il migliore* (the best)! Villagio Inn & Spa is joined by its sister property, the Vintage Inn, on an impeccably designed and centrally-located 23-acre property. Two-story Italian-style Villas span the historic grounds, housing 112 guestrooms and treating its visitors to lovely views of the pristine Domaine Chandon vineyards. Located just alongside the resort's Tuscan-style hillside village is the new 12,000 square-foot Spa Villagio, a facility equipped to fully satisfy any couple's cravings for a weekend of rejuvenation and relaxation.

Together you can experience Spa Villagio's Suite Sensations, a journey into ecstasy for the senses. Choose from Breathe, Awaken, Shine and Together; each suite caters to different desires of the heart, and will pamper you both silly with a colorful array of spa treatments. The Villagio Spa exemplifies the typical leisureliness allowed by the mild California climate: both indoor and outdoor possibilities abound, including a vast swimming pool, tennis courts, and even bicycle rentals. In addition to couple's massages, the resort offers several other features for couples to enjoy together. For example, the "Spa Indulgence" package includes an overnight stay for two in a romantic guestroom, a bottle of fine local wine, a champagne breakfast buffet and your choice of a 50-minute spa treatment for two – try the Wellness Massage or Hydramemory Facial.

In a rave review of the resort, *Town & Country* Magazine describes Villagio Inn & Spa as a "Sybarite's Heaven." Sybaris, an ancient Italian city, has long been known to embody a passionate dedication to uninterrupted pleasure and unsurpassed comfort. I would certainly say that the comparison is an appropriate one – you may very well lose all sense of time and space here, as you drown in shared relaxation and uninhibited indulgences.

VILLAGIO INN & SPA

6481 Washington Street
Yountville, CA 94599
707.944.8877
www.villagio.com

VINTAGE INN

A pure vintage blend of old and new, this French Country-style inn sets the precise tone for ageless romance. A sister to the lovely Villagio Inn & Spa, it is conveniently set in the walking town of Yountville, along the row of world–renowned restaurants often referred to as the "Left Bank" in wine country. Plentiful fine dining awaits you here, including several fantastic French eateries which beckon you to *se faire plasir* for as long as you and your darling please. *Sunset Magazine* calls this place "an inn that is more like a French Chateau," while *First Impressions* Magazine declares it "Unashamedly Romantic....Eighty Guestrooms of sheer luxury and fine taste."

Echoes of 19th Century Romanticism are everywhere. Be transported to Provence by the sensuous French fabrics and decor, attractive French doors leading to your own balcony or patio, and breathtaking views of hillside vineyards. Relax fully in the sunken whirlpool bathtub, then cozy up to the private fireplace in your plush bathrobes and raise your glasses of complimentary wine to celebrate the magic of love. Naturally, a champagne breakfast buffet and afternoon tea are an essential part of the Vintage Inn experience, and it would be a major *faux pas* to pass them up.

Reserve your "Wine Country Romance Getaway" package in advance, and delight in the additional benefits to your stay. The packages vary from season to season, including deluxe accommodations for two, the decadent champagne breakfast, and a chilled bottle of champagne delivered on cue. The concierge can facilitate any added personal touches – including a wedding! The newly-constructed Pavilion at The Vintage Estates serves as a picture-perfect backdrop for your ceremony. In a more casual mood, you may also choose the "Midweek Escape Package" to avoid the crowds and delight in being the only two hand in hand around town. In this French-inspired colorful *bourgade* populated by talented artisans, winemakers, chefs, and painters, you and your loved one will feel no shame in public displays of amour.

VINTAGE INN

6541 Washington St
Yountville, CA 94599
707.944.1112
www.vintageinn.com

WINE COUNTRY INN

G uests celebrate love, pleasure and passion at this intimate retreat, whose sole focus is true romance. Opened in 1975, the Wine Country Inn originally banned phones and television so as to reduce the possibilities for outside distractions from one another and the beautiful shared experience; there are still no televisions on the property, but you definitely won't miss them! The aim here is for couples to find natural romance and peace in the countryside. Many engagements, elopements and romantic rendezvous have subsequently found themselves unfolding in this tranquil lovers' retreat.

Seductive seclusion absorbs you at the Wine Country Inn. Set upon a lovely knoll in St. Helena surrounded by nothing but endless vineyards and lush gardens, the Inn provides Old World charm with modern touches. With only 20 guestrooms, 4 suites and 5 luxury cottages, there is ample room for unmatched personal attention. The helpful concierge, restaurant shuttle service, daily wine tasting from small local wineries, and servings of the owner's fantastic homemade salsa, when available, are just a few examples of the kindnesses extended to couples. The rooms do not disappoint, offering lovely outdoor views, private fireplaces, king or queen-size beds, and a whirlpool or Jacuzzi bathtub; each one is stylishly decorated and exudes its own unique personality. The Wine Country Inn experience is a favorite of *Bon Appétit* writer Hank Rubin, and was chosen as a favorite among the *Best Places to Kiss* collection.

The Inn has come up with some particularly clever and pleasurable romantic packages for you to enjoy. "The Thoughtful Husband" Wife Pampering Package, for example, gives husbands the opportunity to "Break Even," get "Out of the Doghouse," or secure "The Sure Thing," by choosing from a variety of welcoming gifts, spa treatments, breakfast in bed, and other mind-blowing luxuries she'll never be able to say no to. There is also the "Special Occasion Amenities Package" intended to help you "celebrate, rekindle, reconnect." This could include a candlelit dessert for two in your room, lovely arrival and departure gifts, and even silken rose petal trails to guide you further into the heart of unfettered romance.

WINE COUNTRY INN

1152 Lodi Lane
St Helena, CA 94574
707.963-7077
www.winecountryinn.com

Chapter 7

ROMANTIC VIGNETTES

RESTAURANTS

FARM AT CARNEROS INN

ANGÈLE

This intimate restaurant and bar is a hungry lover's paradise. Tucked away within the Historic Napa Mill in Downtown Napa, Angèle is known for its consistently delicious fusion of traditional French cuisine and contemporary influences, as well as its graciously relaxing atmosphere. Angèle is the culmination of the prominent Rouas Family's combined expertise in the hospitality industry. Claude Rouas is the renowned restaurateur and founder of the legendary Auberge du Soleil in Rutherford, as well as the highly-regarded L'Étoile in Nob Hill. His daughters, Bettina and Claudia, climbed on board to lend their skilled hands to the task of creating an exquisite yet low-key French dining establishment in the Napa Valley. The idea for the restaurant was born out of Bettina's inspired stay in Paris, where she lived above a restaurant of the same heavenly name.

This jewel of a restaurant is perched just above the Napa River, and boasts an elegant bistro-style interior dining room and scenic outdoor terrace overlooking the Napa River. All-day service allows guests to visit for an early *déjeuner*, a late-afternoon post-tasting snack, or a romantic dinner. My favorite time to go is in the middle of the day; lounging in the sun on the terrace and savoring a lunch of "Croque Monsieur" (Parisian Ham and Gruyère on Country Bread, Green Salad) with a side of "Gratin de Macaroni," rounding out my tantalizing meal with a tasty glass of sparkling wine. And don't forget the divine desserts – especially the "Chocolat Fondant" (warm chocolate cake with smooth vanilla bean ice cream), *Ooh la la!*

In the evening, the charming full bar and cozy dining room offer a pleasurable space in which to spend a few deliciously intimate hours. Fresh cut flowers adorn every corner, and green petite olive trees sit primly upon each table. The rustic French décor makes for simple, modern elegance, and casual attire is encouraged. *The San Francisco Chronicle*'s Michael Bauer describes Angèle as a "casual brasserie, but one that doesn't skimp on comfort or refinement." The Rouas Family considers a restaurant to be "where one goes to escape from the day-to-day routine," and they have certainly achieved that sensibility here. Indeed, Angèle embodies the true spirit of *joie de vivre* in Wine Country.

ANGÈLE

540 Main Street
Napa, CA 94559
707.252.8115
www.angelerestaurant.com

BISTRO DON GIOVANNI

Owned by Donna and Giovanni Scala, Bistro Don Giovanni is a stylish and immensely popular restaurant and bar in Napa. The colorful menu is overseen by Chef Donna, who focuses on delightful creations with an "Italian and Country French flavor." Utilizing a traditional wood-burning stove and fresh seasonal produce often harvested from the restaurant's abundant on-site garden, Bistro Don Giovanni serves up mouth-watering cuisine and a chic atmosphere which has attracted many loyal patrons over the years.

Surrounded by lush vineyards and a colorful, beautifully-landscaped garden, Don Giovanni expresses the essence of a traditional Mediterranean bistro. High ceilings, elaborate floral arrangements, bistro-style chairs, and bright yellows paired with mellow greens give way to a casually romantic environment. Along the back wall, an open kitchen gives patrons a sneak peak at the beautiful chaos going on behind the scenes. The lively bar adds buzz and pop to the contemporary atmosphere.

Choose between two outdoor terraces for your al fresco dining pleasure; both offer an outdoor fireplace and heaters for cozy romance, but the Northern end also provides tranquil views of the surrounding mountains and the restaurant's whimsical gardens. The garden centerpiece is a lively fountain with life-size artwork depicting characters from "Commedia del Arte." The garden is also host to many essential house ingredients, including home-cured olives pressed and bottled for you to take home as a savory souvenir. If it's possible to squeeze into the popular bar or dine al fresco at one of the highly-desirable terrace tables, there is nothing better than Bistro Don Giovanni's fresh caesar salad, fritto misto, ravioli with lemon crème and variety of classic pizzas. Rounded out by a signature cocktail or glass of fine Napa vintage, this is a quality multinational dining experience made for sharing with the one you love. So . . . *Salute et Bon Appétit!*

BISTRO DON GIOVANNI

4110 Howard Lane
Napa, CA 94558
707.224.3300
www.bistrodongiovanni.com

BISTRO JEANTY

Amust for Francophiles, this quaint French country bistro serves up hearty, authentic *cuisine française* in a warm and unpretentious atmosphere. The restaurant is owned by Chef Philippe Jeanty, a friendly and hospitable Frenchman passionate about expressing his "life-long love affair with food" for the enjoyment of others. Growing up in the Champagne region, Jeanty learned great respect for quality farming and harvesting methods from garden to table; he also began his culinary education at home, under his *Maman* and *Grandmère*. His professional training began at the tender age of 14 at the famous Moet & Chandon Champagne House. After immigrating to Napa Valley to help them establish the Chandon Restaurant, Jeanty decided to recreate the same epicurean delights of his boyhood in the charming town of Yountville.

Shortly after its 1998 debut, Bistro Jeanty's accolades came pouring in, including "Best New Restaurant" awards from the James Beard Foundation and the *San Francisco Chronicle's* Michael Bauer. Dressed in classic French décor and offering a home-style menu, Bistro Jeanty ensures that you will experience "the best French outside France." The restaurant prides itself on remaining informal despite its high-quality fare; the cheerful interior palette, warm lighting and cozy fireplace set the tone for light-hearted romance. Take a seat at the family-style table at the front of the restaurant; if seating is limited, grab a spot on the patio, two seats at the bar, or simply reserve your desired table in advance.

Each and every dish reflects Chef Jeanty's philosophy of fine home-style cuisine, implementing only "fresh quality ingredients, with exacting and demanding preparation." The Pommes Frites are an absolute must, served in the traditional French manner -- perfectly salted and delicately placed into a cone-shaped basket. *J'adore* the warm Crêpe Suzette with orange butter, the Cassoulet (baked beans, duck confit, sausage and bacon) and Coq au Vin (chicken, mushrooms, bacon, and red wine stew) No matter which delicious options you choose, you and your *amant* will enjoy a refreshingly down-to-earth and intimate dining experience at this gem of a bistro.

BISTRO JEANTY

6510 Washington Street
Yountville, CA 94599
707.944.0103
www.bistrojeanty.com

BOUCHON

"One cannot think well, love well, sleep well, if one has not dined well."

- Virginia Woolf

This place embodies a truly Parisian vibe, with authentic French bistro décor and an impressive yet understated menu. All of this adds up to yet another Thomas Keller sensation. A highly-revered chef and owner of the famous French Laundry, Keller is intent on creating memorable dining experiences that last a lifetime. His Bouchon achievement is no exception to this rule. Named after a traditional Lyon bistro, it is affectionately reminiscent of the intimate neighborhood eatery, serving "simple, traditional dishes in a home-like atmosphere." The restaurant successfully transcends time and space to recreate this experience in Napa Valley.

Ever since it first opened its doors in 1998, Bouchon has drawn celebrities, enthusiastic local residents and a slew of "Foodies" from near and far. Each comes with an expectation for the certain *je ne sais quoi* consistent with the neighboring French Laundry. In this more casual and leisurely environment, guests float away holding memories worthy of sharing.

Boasting impeccably-paired food and wine combinations using handcrafted wine exclusively made for Bouchon, the restaurant has received substantial recognition, including three stars from the *San Francisco Chronicle*. Keller highlights his personal excitement and passion for good food in his popular Bouchon cookbook, including a variety of indulgent recipes straight from the menu. Most patrons enjoy sitting on the patio or at the raw bar to savor the Rillettes aux Deux Saumons (fresh & smoked salmon rillettes with toasted croutons), Frisée aux Lardons et Oeuf Poche (frisee salad with bacon lardoons, poached egg, bacon vinaigrette & toasted brioche), or the hugely popular Steak frites and Croque Madame. Don't miss out on this wonderful place, where you will be welcomed by experienced, knowledgeable staff eager to meet your most romantic and sensual dining desires.

BOUCHON

6534 Washington Street
Yountville, CA 94599
707.944.8037
www.bouchonbistro.com

CUVÉE

This hip Napa restaurant and bar provides the perfect backdrop for any dining occasion. Whether you are seeking a light appetizer and robust cocktail or want a swanky, comfortable place for a larger group, this is the right spot. Like its name, Cuvée is all about the art of blending the best elements to achieve universal pleasure. Chef Octavio Barrera has crafted a menu reflecting tasteful American favorites complemented by characteristic Wine Country flare. Signature dishes include Braised Short ribs, Pan-Roasted Chicken and delectable Fresh Fish entrées.

The consistently popular full bar, great cocktails, scrumptious cuisine, fun atmosphere and modern adornment culminate in a wonderful evening at Cuvée. The Premier Cru and Grand Cru Rooms are perfect for a gathering of your entire personal entourage, so reserve in advance. Cozy up next to the warm fireplace and enjoy local live music hosted here several nights a week. Lounge specials and a buzzing Happy Hour are offered as well as an appealing late-night menu serving Lacquered BBQ Pork Ribs and Sushi Grade Ahi Tuna Tartare. On a warm evening, relax under the beautifully-lit patio trees as the sound of live music resonates outside.

Most restaurants in Napa do a great job of providing harmonious food and wine combinations, but Cuvee is especially excellent at food-pairing, using both local and international wines. There is a constant sommelier on hand for helpful recommendations. The restaurant and bar is also host to many seasonal events, such as "Cuvée's Winter Fireside Food and Wine Series," which focuses on the finest products of local wineries and fresh seasonal produce. On the third Wednesday of each month, Cuvee even offers a "three for thirty" special with no corkage -- truly a mid-week treat! On special occasions, order a "Cuvée Gem," a vintage exclusive wine to complete the evening in style, such as the 2002 Joseph Phelps, Insignia, or the 1993 Frog's Leap, Napa Valley. There is so much to indulge in here -- so come on over to one of the liveliest joints in town and lounge the night away together, Wine Country-style.

CUVÉE
1650 Soscol Avenue
Napa, CA 94559
707.224.2330
www.cuveenapa.com

FARM

Part of the luxurious Carneros Inn, FARM provides a polished setting with a wine country *laissez-faire* demeanor. This highly-regarded restaurant and bar shares the resort property with two other dining establishments, the Boon Fly Cafe and the Hilltop Dining Room. However, you need not be a guest at the Carneros Inn to feel welcome at this hip locale. Executive Chef Jeff Jake and Chef de Cuisine Christophe Gerard have joined forces to craft a menu that utilizes organic and sustainable local agriculture and reflects "our commitment to simple, elegant food." The winning combination of sleek designs, trendy-progressive vibes, and fresh, scrumptious food have had critics, locals and tourists raving ever since its conception.

Under beautiful cathedral ceilings in the main dining room, a bona fide romantic lunch or dinner awaits you. All the decadent dishes, including the "Roasted Sonoma Poultry Half Chicken" and "Hens of the Woods Mushroom Risotto" are made to woo you – and they will. For a more casual approach, try the "Farm Certified Angus and Point Reyes Cheeseburger" or "Wood Stone Oven Pizza" from the bar menu. Cozy up on the plush royal blue velvet seating surrounding the bar area, or step outside and unwind for a while in FARM's alfresco living room, featuring comfortable lounge chairs and an attractive modern-style outdoor fire pit, all of which feel characteristic of a carefree overseas hideaway.

Indulging in the tempting offerings of FARM is in fact a virtuous choice; the flagship restaurant has long been dedicated to progressive, environmentally and socially-conscious practices, which they have incorporated into the natural flow of the place with seamless expertise. According to Erika Lenkert of *California Homes Magazine*, Executive Chef Jake "has long been committed to working with the best local, in-season products in a way that respects and celebrates their intrinsic flavors and the environment—and makes for great wine pairing." FARM's innovative menu, glamorous yet relaxed atmosphere, and world-class location result in a memorable Shangri-la dining experience you will no doubt want to make a repeat affair.

FARM RESTAURANT AT CARNEROS INN

4048 Sonoma Highway
Napa, CA 94559
707.299.4880
www.thecarnerosinn.com

Truly the local favorite, Hurley's restaurant offers fantastic wine country cuisine in an upscale environment, without all the associated fuss. Bob Hurley and his General Manager, Jerry Lampe, take a down-to-earth approach to the fine art of the restaurant business. In a valley where chefs are kings, Bob and Jerry welcome each visitor warmly, remain genuinely approachable to all, and are attentive to the input of knowledgeable locals. After nearly two decades in the Valley working at respected establishments, Bob was inspired to open his own restaurant in 2002. His aim was to create an authentic Napa Valley regional cuisine with a subtle Mediterranean twist. Bob always succeeds in producing a menu that any world traveler will delight in by varying the content throughout the year and focusing on fresh, seasonal specialties.

The chic interior dining area at Hurley's is sleek and comfortable, with a leisurely bar frequented by friendly locals. Especially enjoyable is the spacious, heated, and newly-renovated outdoor patio overlooking the colorful central downtown area; this spot is a favorite of mine for simply hanging out and enjoying the lively scenery. The bar offers an extensive cocktail list and an enticing late-night menu, featuring tempting tidbits like Bob's signature Braised Wild Boar Sliders with Wicked Spiced O-Rings. Day or night, Hurley's is the perfect place to kick back and let your appetite do the talking.

Hurley's wine program is an instrumental part of the restaurant. Here, a true wine country dining experience means that the wine is weighed equally with the food, as opposed to pairing as an afterthought. Many Napa Valley winemakers are among Bob's most avid fans, and have made Hurley's their local hangout. Mike Grgich of Grgich Hills Cellar, declares that "Bob understands the importance and intricacies of pairing food and wine. He executes each meal with a balanced palate, so that every taste of food invites the next taste of wine." What better accolades could a wine country chef receive? Named a "Shining Star Chef" by *Cooking Light Magazine,* Bob Hurley continues to build upon his delicious legacy as the owner of the local's ultimate mecca for affairs of the palate.

HURLEY'S RESTAURANT & BAR

6518 Washington Street
Yountville, CA 94599
707.944.2345
www.hurleysrestaurant.com

MARTINI HOUSE

This artfully seductive restaurant and bar is sure to sweep you both off your feet . . . and into a cozy table by one of the blazing stone fireplaces. Owned by famed designer and restaurateur Pat Kuleto and nationally-acclaimed Executive Chef Todd Humphries, the historic Martini House is a hopeless romantic's sanctuary. Voted "One of the Best Restaurants in the World for Wine Lovers" by *Wine Spectator* and called "One of the most romantic places to eat in the Bay Area" by the *San Francisco Chronicle's* Michael Bauer, the Martini House is one-in-a-million.

Originally shared for over fifty years by renowned Opera Singer Walter Martini and his wife, Dionisia, the Martini House has long been an exemplary haven for hospitality, a champion of fine cuisine, and a refuge for wine lovers -- even during the Prohibition years. A delightful variety of unique dining contexts are offered within this craftsman-style bungalow dating back to the 1920s, including the warmly-lit downstairs cellar bar, lovely outdoor garden seating, and a charming main dining room. If you go for the outdoor dining option, expect impeccably landscaped gardens, a koi pond, sprawling fig tree, vine-covered trellises, and myriad flower varieties. The space is simply overflowing with romance.

The Martini House is wonderful no matter what time of year you visit. During winter months, it takes on the feel of a cozy mountain ski lodge, and during the summer, it is a lush, leisurely bungalow. Additionally, Executive Chef Todd Humphries is famous for providing reasons to rejoice in the bounty of every new season, creating what *Zagat* calls "thoughtful, inventive New American dishes of locally foraged ingredients." These include rare elements from the on-site garden, such as black chanterelles, rosehips, juniper berries, wood sorrel, and forest ferns, as well as other fresh organic produce and meats. An especially extravagant choice is provided by the mushroom tasting menu. Guests find Humphries' style fascinating and of superior quality, myself included. The Martini House is without a doubt an experience to be savored, celebrated, and revisited year after year.

MARTINI HOUSE
1245 Spring Street
St Helena, CA 94574
707.963.2233
www.martinihouse.com

RISTORANTE ALLEGRIA

Widely considered a fun romantic refuge by locals, this charming and delicious Italian gem is housed within the dignified former Bank Building, a Napa Historical Landmark. The centrally-located, relatively new restaurant and bar quickly became a regular watering-hole and reliable wining-and-dining spot for locals and visitors in the know. America's most popular reference for great restaurants, the *Zagat Guide*, says that "Napa's Newest Italian has one of the most dramatic settings in the neighborhood… The Cuisine showcases some old favorites and some not-so-Italian variations…With such good food and friendly service…it's sure to be a hit." After just one night here together, I suspect you will most certainly agree!

Ristorante Allegria is one of the most seductive spots in Downtown Napa for its fabulous menu, unique atmosphere, and stellar service. Highlighting the best of Northern-Italian cuisine complemented by a colorful California twist, Ristorante Allegria's popular chef prepares three specialty dishes each day utilizing purely fresh, seasonal ingredients. The Napa Cabbage Salad, Wild Mushroom Ravioli and Marinated Grilled Teriyaki Skirt Steak will satisfy anyone's culinary desires. Once dessert time rolls around, the bread pudding is not to be missed. The popular Box Lunches also make for a quick and convenient lunchtime treat in style.

The historic Bank Building features high, beautifully ornate ceilings, a quiet, private "vault" dining room for private parties and special occasions, and comfortable outdoor seating with heat lamps. Every interior detail is sure to please, including polished candlelit tables, romantic lighting, excellent and famously attentive service, an open kitchen, and a full bar with signature cocktails. For Chef's Market, a lively Summer event during which the Napa downtown area is closed to traffic and filled with live bands and wine tasting tables, nearly everyone crowds into Allegria for a celebratory dinner. On Mondays and Wednesdays, you will be serenaded by live accordion music. In truth, you can never go wrong with a visit to the *magnifico* Ristorante Allegria!

RISTORANTE ALLEGRIA

1026 1st Street
Napa, CA 94559
707.254.8006
www.ristoranteallegria.com

Ristorante Allegria WINE BAR

Ristorante
Allegria

1026 First St. Napa

Phone
707.254.8006

jaimefritsch.com

UVA TRATTORIA ITALIANA

This lively Napa downtown hotspot is as popular with locals as it is with tourists. Featuring classic Southern-Italian dishes, such as Calamari Fritti, Gnocchi al Gorgonzola and Pollo Arrosto con Limone, Uva is a vibrant restaurant for live jazz music, a cocktail rendezvous, a fun and appetizing dinner or just a casual lunch. Owners Sean Pramuk and Giovanni Guerrera, who celebrated six jammin' years in April 2008, have successfully achieved their goal of creating a hip and friendly atmosphere. Winning local supporters, weathering the dreaded Napa floods, and maintaining consistently popular nightlife entertainment is no easy feat in downtown Napa. But with the recent growth in the Downtown area, a new flood control plan, and an adoring local fan base, Uva has secured its spot as the go-to meeting point and local music venue.

Chef Giovanni Guerrera calls his version of rustic Italian cuisine "cucina casareccia: home-cooked soul-satisfying meals without the pretense of haute dining." The menu also offers fresh salads, seasonal creations and traditional Italian pizzas. Uva even grows most of its own vegetables at Scully Ranch near Napa's Mount Veeder. Their garden curator, Rick, harvests and delivers fresh organic produce on the same day, and collaborates with Giovanni to grow environmentally sustainable crops. "We are so fortunate to be able to live in an area that can afford us this luxury," says Giovanni.

Five nights a week, Uva offers live jazz, most notably Philip Smith and the Gentlemen of Jazz, a favorite local band, with special guests appearing on Saturday evenings. The music radiates through the whole restaurant, creating a jovial vibe. "The city of Napa rolls up its sidewalks after dark, but Uva makes an exception . . . Photos of old jazz greats crowd the walls, and you can tap along from the swanky dining room or the crowded bar." Many revelers mingle at the bar, sipping cocktails and enjoying a small plate from the tasty late-night menu on Friday and Saturday nights. Join the fun on the impromptu dance floor, and twirl the night away together in this pitch-perfect downtown venue.

UVA TRATTORIA ITALIANA

1040 Clinton Street
Napa, CA 94559
707.255.6646
www.uvatrattoria.com

Chapter 8

CREATING ROMANCE

ADVICE FROM LOCAL WEDDING PLANNER,
SUZY BERBERIAN

NAPA VALLEY WINE TRAIN

ADVICE FROM LOCAL WEDDING PLANNER, SUZY BERBERIAN, ON CREATING A MAGICAL ENGAGEMENT

Demanding Bridezillas, nervous grooms, and high-maintenance celebrities are all part of Suzy Berberian's daily job as Wedding Coordinator Extraordinaire. A self-described "hopeless romantic," beautiful weddings are Suzy's passion. Not only does she create, produce and coordinate exquisite weddings, but as a certified Sommelier, she even makes knowledgeable choices for the most appropriate and tantalizing wines to complete the memory – only in Napa Valley!

Suzy started her career in romantic unions at the luxurious Auberge du Soleil, and has assisted over 400 couples in planning and pulling off their own definition of a perfect wedding. She has recently branched out to work with A Dream Wedding, where she focuses completely on making your dreams for this memorable day into a reality. Known for her flawless service, attention to detail and endless patience, Suzy is simply the best possible source for ideas to create magical moments in Napa Valley that neither one of you will ever forget.

SUZY BERBERIAN
Wedding Planner

Q 4.7 million people visit Napa Valley every year, and 80% of them are couples. Why do so many couples visit, get engaged, and marry here?

A In a word: romance! Napa Valley has a really unique mix of things that draw couples here: beautiful views, world-class food and wine, and luxurious hotels. It is the perfect place to visit as a new couple, become engaged, marry or honeymoon. I know many couples that were married in the Napa Valley so they could return every year for their anniversary celebration.

Q What is the best Napa Valley proposal a couple has shared with you?

A The best proposal I've heard of was actually one that I helped plan! The couple was sharing a romantic lunch at the Auberge du Soleil, overlooking the vineyards of Napa Valley, and the gentleman asked her to marry him near the end of the meal. He then led her downstairs to the Private Terrace, where both of their families had gathered to surprise her and toast the couple. He had secretly arranged for the entire group to fly in for the weekend. They spent the next two hours celebrating the couple, taking photos, and enjoying champagne, local artisan cheeses and chocolate-covered strawberries.

Q Personally, what places do you find the most romantic in Napa Valley?

A My husband and I love to spend time in Napa Valley, and some of our favorite romantic places are:
• Martini House, St. Helena: the downstairs bar is cozy, with low-lighting and a giant fireplace. There is no better place on a rainy day for a romantic lunch (with wine, of course).
• Swanson Vineyards, Oakville: This boutique winery features amazing wine, and it has an intimate tasting "salon" with a table for eight guests. You truly feel like you are in Paris with the beautiful chandelier and fireplace setting the scene for a delicious cheese and wine pairing.
• Auberge du Soleil, Rutherford: This is absolutely the most romantic hotel in the area. The luxurious rooms have stunning views of the entire valley, and the spa has "couples" rooms with private baths and outdoor showers. It's heaven here in Napa Valley.

Q   What is the most romantic celebration you have created for a couple?

A   To me, the most romantic weddings are when special touches are added to honor the couple and their history together. One couple started with a traditional American wedding ceremony, and then invited all the guests inside to share in a traditional Persian ceremony. The heritage of both the bride and groom were honored and celebrated. Another bride arranged for a bagpipe processional, because she met her fiancé while going to school in Ireland. Romance is definitely in the details.

Q   Beyond food & wine, what are some other romantic activities a couple can experience in Napa Valley?

A   If you don't mind waking up early, a hot air balloon ride over the Napa Valley is adventurous, energizing and beautiful! After floating peacefully across the valley you and your partner can enjoy a romantic champagne brunch. For a more relaxing day, couples can arrange for spa treatments at a number of local day spas. Solage Calistoga has a Mud Bar, and you can book a treatment to paint each other with local volcanic mud before soaking in natural geo-thermal spring water.

Q   If a couple had only one day in Napa, how would you recommend that they spend it?

A   Try to visit for longer than one day if you can! With one day I would recommend visiting a sparkling wine house for a leisurely morning tasting, followed by lunch at one of the more casual local restaurants (Hurley's, Rutherford Grill or Market). After lunch visit one more winery featuring your favorite type of wine, then take a shopping stroll through one of the wonderful towns in the valley – Yountville, St. Helena or Calistoga. For dinner, there are a number of amazing restaurants, so pick one you've been dying to try and feast on the world-famous cuisine and wine of Napa Valley!

Top Ten Napa Valley Proposals

1. Be creative – ask a server at one of the recommended romantic restaurants to write "Will you marry me?" in chocolate sauce around the plate of your lover's dessert, and pop the question as they bring it out to the table. Make sure to have a bottle of champagne on hand to celebrate.

2. Sail together in a hot air balloon over the crisp and dewy vineyards as the sun rises, on a ride arranged only for you two.

3. Bask in the beautiful view at one of the suggested romantic wineries, such as Artesa or Rutherford Hill; take a chance as the sun begins to set, perhaps on bended knee.

4. Hop on the Napa Valley Wine Train and explore the Valley "Old World" style in a luxurious private booth; let the magic of traditional romance set you both afire.

5. Arrange a private candlelit dinner in a wine cave, perhaps at Meritage or Calistoga Ranch, with our local serenading Spanish Flamenco guitar player, Ben Woods.

6. Horseback ride through Napa's picturesque hillsides and take pleasure in a private picnic afterwards.

7. Relish a sunset, sparkling wine, and one of the best views in the Valley on the renowned Auberge du Soleil patio.

8. Hike to the top of Mount St. Helena on a crisp morning in Robert Louis Stevenson Park; once you reach the top have lunch ready and savor the heavenly view together.

9. Charter a private helicopter ride over the Valley for a breathtaking proposal!

10. Splurge on the dinner of a lifetime at the irresistible French Laundry, and propose between the many delectable courses.

CHAPTER TWO RESOURCES

NAPA

Back Room Wines
974 Franklin Street
Napa, CA 94559
707.226.1378
www.backroomwines.com

Cole's Chop House
1122 Main Street
Napa, CA 94559
707.224.6328
www.coleschophouse.com

Copia: The American Center
for Wine, Food, & the Arts
500 1st Street
Napa, CA 94559
707.259.1600
888.512.6742
707.257.8601 fax
www.copia.org

Julia's Kitchen
500 1st Street
Napa, CA 94559
707.265.5700
www.copia.org
www.opentable.com

Napa Mill
500 Main Street
Napa, CA 94559
707.252.9372
www.napariverinn.com/
napamill.php

Celadon
500 Main Street # G
Napa, CA 94559
707.254.9690
www.celadonnapa.com

Hatt Building
500 Main Street
Napa, CA 94559

Napa General Store
540 Main Street
Napa, CA 94559
707.259.0762
napageneralstore.com

Sweetie Pies
520 Main Street
Napa, CA 94559
707.257.7280
www.sweetiepies.com

Napa Valley Opera House
1030 Main Street
Napa, CA 94559
707.226.7372
770.226.5392 fax
www.napavalleyoperahouse.org

Oxbow Public Market
644 1st Street
Napa, CA 94559
707.226.6529
oxbowpublicmarket.com

Kitchen Library
707.253.1894
www.stevenrothfeld.com

Rocca Family Vineyards
1130 Main Street
Napa, CA 94559
707.257.8467
www.roccawines.com

Ubuntu Restaurant & Yoga
1140 Main Street
Napa, CA 94559
707.251.5656
www.ubuntunapa.com

Vintner's Collective
1245 Main Street
Napa, CA 94559
707.255.7150
www.vintnerscollective.com

YOUNTVILLE

Bouchon Bakery
6528 Washington Street
Yountville, CA 94599
707.944.2253
www.frenchlaundry.com

French Laundry Restaurant
6640 Washington Street
Yountville, CA 94599
707.944.2380
www.frenchlaundry.com

Lincoln Theatre
100 California Drive
Yountville, CA 94599
707.944.1300
www.lincolntheatre.org

Napa Valley Museum
55 Presidents Circle
Yountville, CA 94599
707.944.0500
www.napavalleymuseum.org

Pacific Blues Café
6525 Washington Street
Yountville, CA 94599
707.944.4455
www.pacificbluescafe.com

Veterans Home of
California –Yountville
180 California Drive
Yountville, CA 94599
800.404.8387
www.ca.gov

Vintage 1870
6525 Washington Street
Yountville, CA 94599
707.944.8771
www.vintage1870.com

RUTHERFORD & OAKVILLE

Oakville Grocery
7856 St. Helena Highway
Oakville, CA 94562
707.944.8802
www.oakvillegrocery.com

Opus One Winery
7900 St. Helena Highway
Oakville, CA 94562
707.944.9442
www.opusonewinery.com

Rubicon Estate
1991 St. Helena Highway
Rutherford, CA 94573
707.968.1100
www.rubiconestate.com

Rutherford Grill
1180 Rutherford Road
Rutherford, CA 94573
707.963.1792
www.hillstone.com

Silver Oak Cellars
915 Oakville Cross Road
Oakville, CA 94562
800.273.8809
www.silveroak.com

St. Helena Olive Oil
Company
8576 Saint Helena Highway
Rutherford, CA 94573
707.967.1003
www.sholiveoil.com

ST. HELENA

Bale Grist Mill State Park
3369 Saint Helena Highway
North
St Helena, CA 94574
707.963.2236
www.ca.gov

Beringer Vineyards
2000 Main Street
St Helena, CA 94574
707.967.4412
www.beringer.com

Culinary Institute of
America at Greystone
2555 Main Street
St Helena, CA 94574
707.967.1010
www.ciachef.edu

Meadowood Napa Valley
900 Meadowood Lane
St Helena, CA 94574
707.963.3646
www.meadowood.com

Napa Valley Coffee Roasting
Company
948 Main Street
Napa, CA 94559
707.224.2233
www.napavalleycoffee.com

Taylor's Automatic Refresher
933 Main Street
St Helena, CA 94574
707.963.3486
www.taylorsrefresher.com

CALISTOGA

Buster's Original Southern
BBQ
1207 Foothill Boulevard
Calistoga, CA 94515
707.942.5605
www.busterssouthernbbq.com

Calistoga Farmers Market
1546 Lincoln Avenue
Calistoga, CA 94515
707.942.0808

Calistoga Mineral Water
865 Silverado Trail
Calistoga, CA 94515
707.299.2800
www.calistogawater.com

Dr. Wilkinson's Hot Springs
1507 Lincoln Avenue
Calistoga, CA 94515
707.942.4102
www.drwilkinson.com

Indian Springs Resort & Spa
1712 Lincoln Ave
Calistoga, CA 94515
707.942.4913
www.indianspringscalistoga.com

Robert Louis Stevenson
State Park
3801 Saint Helena Highway
Calistoga, CA 94515
707.942.4575
www.ca.gov

Schramsberg Vineyards
1400 Schramsberg Road
Calistoga, CA 94515
707.942.4558
www.schramsberg.com

CHAPTER THREE RESOURCES

ATTENTION WINE & DOG LOVERS

FRIDAY

The Meritage Resort at Napa
875 Bordeaux Way
Napa, California 94558
707.251.1900
www.themeritageresort.com

Siena Restaurant,
Meritage Resort
707.259.0633
Ristorante Allegria
1026 1st Street
Napa, CA 94559
707.254.8006
www.ristoranteallegria.com

Uva Trattoria Italiana
1040 Clinton Street
Napa, CA 94559
707.255.6646
www.uvatrattoria.com

Bounty Hunter Rare Wine
Company
975 1st Street
Napa, CA 94559
707.226.3976
www.bountyhunterwine.com

Vallerga's Market
3385 Solano Avenue
Napa, CA 94558
707.253.2621
www.vallergas.com

Mumm Napa
8445 Silverado Trail
Napa, CA 94558
707.967.7700
www.mummnapa.com

Regusci Winery
5584 Silverado Trail
Napa, CA 94558
707.254.0403
www.regusciwinery.com

Signorello Vineyards
4500 Silverado Trail
Napa, CA 94558
707.255.5990
www.signorellovineyards.com

Farm Restaurant at Carneros
Inn
4048 Sonoma Highway
Napa, CA 94559
707.299.4880
www.thecarnerosinn.com

SUNDAY

Fume Bistro & Bar
4050 Byway East
Napa, CA 94558
707.257.1999
www.fumebistro.com

Alston Park
2099 Dry Creek Road
Napa, California
707.257.9529

O'Brien Estate Winery
1200 Orchard Avenue
Napa, CA 94558
707.252.8463
www.obrienestate.com

AN EPICUREAN BIKE RIDE THROUGH STAGS LEAP

FRIDAY

Vintage Inn
6541 Washington Street
Yountville, CA 94599
707.944.1112
www.vintageinn.com

Bistro Jeanty
6510 Washington Street
Yountville, CA 94599
707.944.0103
www.bistrojeanty.com

Pancha's of Yountville
6764 Washington Street
Yountville, CA 94599
707.944.2125

SATURDAY

Bouchon Bakery
6528 Washington Street
Yountville, CA 94599
707.944.2253
www.frenchlaundry.com

Napa Valley Bike Tours &
Rentals
6488 Washington Street
Yountville, CA 94599
707.944.2953
www.napavalleybiketours.com

Jessup Cellars, Inc.
6740 Washington Street
Yountville, CA 94599
707.944.8523
www.jessupcellars.com

Robert Sinskey Vineyards
6320 Silverado Trail
Napa, CA 94558
800.869.2030
www.robertsinskey.com

Cliffe Lede Vineyards
1473 Yountville Crossroad
Yountville, CA 94599
707.944.8642

Goosecross Cellars
1119 State Lane
Yountville, CA 94599
707.944.1986
www.goosecross.com

Bistro Don Giovanni
4110 Howard Lane
Napa, CA 94558
707.224.3300
www.bistrodongiovanni.com

CHAPTER THREE RESOURCES

Lincoln Theatre
100 California Drive
Yountville, CA 94599
707.944.1300
www.lincolntheatre.org

Napa Valley Opera House
1030 Main Street
Napa, CA 94559
707.226.7372 &
770.226.5392 fax
www.napavalleyoperahouse.org

SUNDAY

Vintner's Golf Club &
Lakeside Grill
7901 Solano Avenue
Yountville, CA 94599
707.944.2426
www.vintnersgolfclub.com

Domaine Chandon Winery
1 California Drive
Yountville, CA 94599
707.944.2892
www.chandon.com

Étoile Restaurant
800.736.2892

RELAXATION ABOVE THE CLOUDS

FRIDAY

Silverado Country Club
1600 Atlas Peak Road
Napa, CA 94558
707.257.0200
www.silveradoresort.com

SATURDAY

Balloons Above the Valley
603 California Boulevard
Napa, CA 94559
707.253.2222
www.ballonrides.com

Napa General Store
Napa Mill
540 Main Street
Napa, CA 94559
707.259.0762
napageneralstore.com

St. Supery Winery
8440 St Helena Highway
Rutherford, CA 94573
707.963.4507
www.stsupery.com

Milat Winery
1091 Saint Helena Hwy S
St Helena, CA 94574
707.963.0758

Pine Ridge Winery
5901 Silverado Trail
Napa, CA 94558
707.252.9777
www.pineridgewinery.com

Bay Leaf Restaurant
2025 Monticello Rd
Napa, CA 94558
707.257.9720
www.bayleafnapa.com

SUNDAY

Domaine Carneros
1240 Duhig Road
Napa, CA 94559
707.257.0101
www.domaine.com

ENDLESS ROMANCE

FRIDAY

Harvest Inn
1 Main Street
St. Helena, CA 94574
707.963.9463
www.jdvhotels.com

Tra Vigne Restaurant
1050 Charter Oak Avenue
St. Helena, CA 94574
707.963.4444
www.travignerestaurant.com

SATURDAY

Sterling Vineyards
1111 Dunaweal Lane
Calistoga, CA 94515
707.942.3300
www.sterlingvineyards.com

Clos Pegase Winery
1060 Dunaweal Lane
Calistoga, CA 94515
707.942.4981
www.clospegase.com

Castello di Amorosa
4045 Saint Helena Highway
Calistoga, CA 94515
707.942.8200
www.castellodiamorosa.com

Martini House
1245 Spring Street
St Helena, CA 94574
707.963.2233
www.martinihouse.com

Ana's Cantina
1205 Main Street
St Helena, CA 94574
707.963.4921

SUNDAY

Calistoga Spa Hot Springs
1006 Washington Street
Calistoga, CA 94515
707.942.6269
www.calistogaspa.com

Rutherford Grill
1180 Rutherford Road
Rutherford, CA 94573
707.963.1792
www.hillstone.com

Elizabeth Spencer Wines
1165 Rutherford Rd
Rutherford, CA 94573
707.963.6067
www.elizabethspencerwines.com

TOP TEN WINE COUNTRY PROPOSALS INDEX

2. **Napa Valley Balloons, Inc.**
    6795 Washington Street # C
    Yountville, CA 94599
    707.944.0228
    www.napavalleyballoons.com

    Napa Valley Aloft
    6525 Washington St
    Yountville, CA 94599
    707.944.8638
    800.627.2759
    www.nvaloft.com

4. **Napa Valley Wine Train**
    1275 Mckinstry Street
    Napa, CA 94559
    707.253.2160
    www.winetrain.com

5. **Benjamin Woods**
    Flemenco Guitar, Percussion
    benwoods66@yahoo.com

6. **Skyline Wilderness Park**
    2201 Imola Avenue
    Napa, CA 94559
    707.252.0481
    www.ncfaa.com/skyline/skyline_park.htm

    Horseback Riding at Skyline Wilderness Park:
    707.479.8031
    www.napasonomatrailrides.com
    midori@northbaynaturalhorsemanship.com

9. **Wine Country Helicopters**
    2030 Airport Rd
    Napa, CA 94558
    707.226.8470
    www.winecountryhelicopters.com

FEATURED PHOTOGRAPHERS

Andrea MacNamara Jacoby

Co-founder of Winery Dogs Publishing and Photographer for the highly popular *Winery Dogs of Napa Valley* and *Winery Dogs of Sonoma*, Andrea has successfully found a way to combine her three passions: wine, dogs and photography.

PAGES: 18, 19, 39, 66, 67, 156, 157

Eric Zachary Ryder

Eric is a New England native who made his way to Northern California in the mid-80's. His career has offered him the opportunity to travel to locations around the country and pursue his passion for color and infrared photography. Since moving to the Napa Valley in 2001, he's focused mainly on unique images of the Wine Country, using specialized equipment and highly-crafted image processing techniques. The resulting works rarely fail to produce a visceral response from the viewer. Eric's most recent collection, The Illuminated Landscape, is featured at Blue Heron Gallery in Yountville. www.ticket2ryder.com

PAGES: 36, 37, 83, 121, 126, 134, 135, 142, 146, 158

John Klycinski

A Napa native, John works with local couples, businesses and wineries and prides himself on being meticulous and professional to ensure the right shot. With over 15 years of experience, John has traveled the world and is particularly passionate about black and white photography. He is also a Photography Instructor at Sacramento City College.

PAGES: COVER PHOTOGRAPH, 11, 76, 80, 107, 141, 161

Photographs Courtesy of:

1801 First, Luxury Inn
Photography by Jay Graham

Far Niente Winery
Photography by Adrian Gregorutti

Carneros Inn
Cottage Neighborhood
Photography by Art Gary

Carneros Inn
Horses Picture
Photography by Angie Silvy

Kuleto Winery
Napa River Inn
Calistoga Ranch
Meritage Resort
Silverado Resort
Solage
Wine Country Inn

Thank You

Featured Napa Valley businesses for your enduring support; there are too many gracious people to thank individually. It's an honor, and a privilege to live in such a beautiful, neighborly place. Andrea & Allen Jacoby, Winery Dogs of Napa Valley; Christina Luce, writing and editing assistant; Eric Ryder, Photographer; Andrea Jacoby, Photographer; John Klycinski, Photographer; Jaime Fritsch, Photographer; Chris Blanchard, REDD; Bob Hurley, Hurley's Restaurant; Suzy Berberian, A Dream Wedding; Carolynn Gamble, Napa Valley Small Business Center; Eric Marjoram, Michaela Cantwell & J.J. Swann, Houston& Design Team; Marie Millhouse, Inspiration; and all my other family and friends for your love and support.